THE SPELL BOOK OF WICCAN SHADOWS
DAWN FLOWERS

Tazia,

Wishing you the brightest of blessings!

Dawn Flowers

The Spell Book of Wiccan Shadows,
Copyright © Dawna Flowers 2001, 2004, 2011, 2019.

Published by Amazon for Under the Moon Publishing, 2019.
Illustrations Copyright © Shawna Lowman, 2001, 2004, 2011, 2019.
Drawings, & Illustrations Copyright © 2019 Dover Publications.

No part of this book may be reproduced electronically,
or by any means without written permission from the publisher.
All Rights Reserved

9781453753866

Dedicated to the Memory of
REBECCA GREENSMITH

This book is dedicated to the memory of Rebecca Greensmith, my eleventh great-Grandmother, executed for Witchcraft in Hartford County, Connecticut on January 25th, 1662. Her death served as a precursor of tragedies yet to come for the colonies, occurring during the embryonic stage of America's Witch Hunts, thirty years before the tragedies in Salem.

Though we have court records and confessions, we've no way of knowing if she *truly* practiced Witchcraft, or if her confessions were coerced, as many others were. We do know that she died for drinking and dancing with her friends under a moonlit tree, and we might speculate that she was the local Granny Witch, a neighborhood healer of sorts common at the time in Europe and colonial America.

Regardless, she died for being a Witch, whether she was one or not, and for that, her memory and death, along with all the others who perished during the Witch Hunts, both then and now, should remain in our memories as martyrs to our path. May each of their soul's rest and find the peace they were denied in life.

Dearest Reader,

Within, you'll find an assortment of Wiccan spells, remedies, recipes, folk-healing recipes, concoctions, and back-wood brews, along with introductory material explaining common tools, topics, issues, and techniques. Though this book was created for Wiccan practitioners with an emphasis on healing, it can be used by *any* practitioner of Witchcraft and makes a fun tool for anyone exploring the Magical Arts.

My first book, *The Book of Dark & Light Shadows,* explored concepts of Magic which are rightfully prohibited within the Wiccan community. It touches on taboo paths, including Satanism and Voodoo. I wanted to provide an unbiased look into the most common Witchcraft-related occult paths prevalent today, and to help preserve modern interpretations of Witchcraft and Occult practices. I wanted to examine various paths, and with that exploration came many, many spells. Around two-hundred. A portion of those spells were unusable by Wiccan practitioners, as they clearly went against general Wiccan principles. These included a few love spells, a few curses, and a few that dealt with spirit manipulations, ceremonial Magick, etc. Though *The Book of Dark & Light Shadows* was an incredibly fun book to create, I wanted to create a book that better reflected my own Wiccan tendencies, and those of my Wiccan readers. And so, I went back and rewrote the entire book to align with the basic principles within Modern Wicca, and the result is what you're reading, today. There are thirty new spells within this Wiccan edition, which are exclusively for healing and positive Magic. Edits made during 2019 include a dedication to Rebecca Greensmith and a closing essay titled, *Witch Hunts*.

Before we dive in, I'd like to take a moment to thank my sister, Shawna Bowman, for her wonderful artwork and for her support in the creation of this book. I'd also like to thank Ernst & Johanna Lehner and Dover Publications for contributing artwork from, *Devils Demons & Witchcraft*.

Most of all, I'd like to thank *you*, dearest reader, for your interest in my work, and for choosing a most beautiful path to explore. It's my greatest hope that you find this project helpful as you seek to learn about Wiccan philosophies. If you enjoy the material found within these pages, I hope you'll consider leaving a kind review, so that others might know to enjoy it, too.

Brightest of Blessings,
~Dawn Flowers

Table of Contents

7	Introductory Letter from the Author
9	Table of Contents
11	**Part I. Wiccan Basics**
13	Chapter 1. Introduction to Wiccan Concepts
29	Chapter 2. Spell Components & Tools
47	Chapter 3. Times to Perform Magic
57	**Part II. Healing Spells**
59	About the Spells
61	Chapter 4. Cold & Flu
67	Chapter 5. Pain Relieving
71	Chapter 6. Muscle Complaint
75	Chapter 7. Female Concerns
81	Chapter 8. Insomnia
87	Chapter 9. Skin Ailments
95	Chapter 10. Stomach Ailments
101	Chapter 11. Emotional Strain & Stress
107	Chapter 12. Other Mentionable Healing Methods
117	**Part III. Spiritually Enlightening Spells & Concepts**
119	Chapter 13. Divination, Pendulums, Rune Stones
139	Chapter 14. Prophecy, Visions, & Dreaming
145	Chapter 15. Meditation & Astral Travel
149	Chapter 16. Cleansings, Blessings, & Purifications
155	Chapter 17. Seeking Truth & Knowledge
159	**Part IV. General Spells & Concepts**
161	Chapter 18. Protective Measures
169	Chapter 19. Strength and Power
173	Chapter 20. Money
181	Chapter 21. Luck & Wishing
185	Chapter 22. Traveling and Outdoors
189	Chapter 23. Spirits, Ghosts, and Exorcisms
193	Chapter 24. Removing Curses
199	Chapter 25. Other Mentionable Spells
205	**Part V. Additional Material**
207	Witch Hunts, Essay
213	About the Author
214	Bibliography & Recommended Reading

Table of Personal Notations

Use the following Table of Contents to record and keep track of your personal notations. There are blank pages found throughout the book for you to input your own spells, notes, etc. Keep track of your notes for easy referencing later.

Chapter	Content Summary	Page

Part I   Wiccan Basics

Introduction to Wiccan Concepts
Spell Components & Tools
Times to Perform Magic

Chapter 1
Introduction to Wiccan Concepts

Wicca is a peaceful and beautiful path practiced by modern Witches, and is the most popular of the Magical faiths within Witchcraft. Wiccans have a strong code of morality defined by guidelines which vary slightly between coven to coven, but remain faithful to the Wiccan Rede. Each of the spells presented in this book can be practiced with a good conscience and fall well within acceptable forms of Magic as practiced by most Wiccan covens and solitary Wiccan practitioners.

Some of you might already know, a Book of Shadows is a compilation of materials used for one's religious practices within Magic. Traditional Books of Shadows are produced by a Witch or Pagan to collect successful spells, healing practices, divination techniques, personal notes, and any other relevant information which would assist them in their religion, health, relationships, work, and daily life. Various cultural and pharmaceutical studies regarding the healing techniques of early natives around the globe now prove the validity of many of our ancestors' remedies, and so this book is a blending of both traditional and modern healing techniques, some with a touch of scientific backing, though research on herbal use is still very limited, and I urge you to research any herb you use in your Magical practices.

You'll find this a very easy book to use, even if you're fairly new to Wicca. Most of the tools are easily acquired, and the spells are basic, but tried and true. You'll be using this book much like you would a cookbook. Prop it on something and gather up the ingredients you will need for your work, and have fun.

But first, read over the Wiccan Rede, a famous poem, which we all hold dear. It's one of the many versions whose original author remains unknown or disputed, depending on who you ask. A short eight-word couplet version was first recorded in a speech in 1964 by Doreen Valiente, consisting of "An it harm none do what ye will," which was later published to include the following: "Eight words the Wiccan Rede fulfill, An it harm none do what ye will." The Long Rede, as it's sometimes called, was first published in 1974 in a magazine, Earth Religion News. It was published again in 1975 by Green Egg magazine by Phyllis (Lady Gwen) Thompson, as "Rede Of The Wiccae." Thompson credited its original writing to her grandmother, Adriana Porter. The disputed authorship doesn't negate the meaning of its words.

Regardless of who wrote it first, or when, its advice is sound and beautifully put. Its content is every bit as relevant today, as it was sixty-years ago. Most Wiccan followers adhere to most of the advice given within its stanzas, and doing so is what defines Wicca for many people. In fact, many Witches differentiate themselves from Wiccans, because they don't follow the Wiccan Rede to the letter. Some Wiccans are a bit relaxed when it comes to making all of their spells rhyme, as noted in the poem, but for the most part, The Wiccan Rede is our light in the darkness. It's our beacon in the fog. If you question whether what you're doing is right or not, give the Rede a read, and think about your situation before acting. Let it be your guide on a road that's paved with good actions, not just good intentions. If you listen, if can help you do the right thing, in everything.

    The Rede encourages good behaviors, a healthy mentality, a positive mindset, and of course, good Magic. It discourages negativity and warns strongly of its repercussions, with the rule of three. Whatever you do, good or bad, will come back to you three times. I believe this to be true, even if you take Magic out of the equation. I believe if you do good things, it creates an environment for good things to return, and many believe that is the core of Wicca, creating good.

Wiccan Rede

Bide the Wiccan Laws we must,
In perfect Love and Perfect Trust.

Live and let live,
Fairly take and fairly give.

Cast the Circle thrice about,
To keep the evil spirits out.

To bind the spell every time,
Let the spell be spoke in rhyme.

Soft of eye and light of touch,
Speak little, listen much.

Deosil go by the waxing moon,
Chanting out the Witches' Rune.

Widdershins go by the waning-moon,
Chanting out the baneful rune.

When the lady's moon is new,
Kiss the hand to her, times two.

When the moon rides at her peak,
Then your heart's desire seek.

Heed the North wind's mighty gale,
Lock the door and drop the sail.

When the wind comes from the South,
Love will kiss thee on the mouth.

When the wind blows from the West,
Departed souls will have no rest.

When the wind blows from the East,
Expect the new and set the feast.

Nine woods in the cauldron go,
Burn them fast and burn them slow.

Elder be the Lady's tree,
Burn it not or cursed you'll be.

When the Wheel begins to turn,
Let the Beltane fires burn.

When the Wheel has turned to Yule,
Light the logs and Horned one rules.

Heed ye Flowers, Bush and Tree,
By the Lady, blessed be.

When the rippling waters go,
Cast a stone and truth you'll know.

When ye have a true need,
Hearken not to other's greed.

With a fool no season spend,
Lest ye be counted as his friend.

Merry meet and merry part,
Bright the cheeks and warm the heart.

Mind the Threefold Law you should,
Three times bad and three times good.

When misfortune is enow,
Wear the blue star on thy brow.

True is love ever be,
Lest thy lover's false to thee.

Eight words the Wiccan Rede fulfill,
An' Harm ye none, do as you will.

Witchcraft & Wicca

Defining Witchcraft can be tricky, since its connotations vary wildly depending on the country, state, or neighborhood. One person's *superstitions* might be another's *Witchcraft*. But, when I think of Witchcraft in general, I think of two distinct forms. There's *Witchcraft - the religion,* and then there's *Witchcraft - the label,* used derogatorily to make allegations that discredit, condemn, punish, imprison, or execute someone, whether true or false.

Both forms have one thing in common, and that's a belief that people or circumstances can be manipulated through working with a higher force, or as it's sometimes called, *Magic*. Whether someone is a practicing Witch, or whether someone is accusing someone of being a practicing Witch, in both cases the different parties involved believe in Magic, though with two distinctly different opinions of the practice.

Contrary to popular misconceptions, Magic isn't exclusive to Witchcraft. Christian, Jewish, and Muslim prayers fit the description for Magic, but most of them reject the term, or use it derogatorily. There are scholars who study the Magic of religiously revered people including Christ, Allah, Buddha, Moses, and others, but Mysticism and Esoteric studies aren't the average folk's cup of tea, and so Magic is perceived by many as deviant, when in all actuality, it's the foundation of *every* functioning religion that exists today, and throughout the history of mankind. Even Atheism wouldn't exist without Magic, as there'd be nothing for followers to reject.

When I think of Witchcraft, I think of *many* paths including Wicca, Santeria, Voodoo, Hoodoo, Ceremonial Magick, and a bit of Christian and Jewish Mysticism, but the scope is much larger and there are forms of it stretching around the globe. Every country has its own brand, and some countries have many.

Witchcraft in America is a little different than European Witchcraft, and includes not only European influences, but heavy doses of Native American, Hispanic, Caribbean, African, Middle Eastern, and Asian influences, resulting in a variety of intermingled, globally infused paths.

This blending of paths in North American Witchcraft took root in the 1600's as immigrants, slaves, and indentured servants made their way from Europe, Africa, and the Caribbean during early colonization to the Americas. These varied paths absorbed Native American influences including herbalism, shamanistic healing, and communion with ancestral spirits. Through the years, each of these paths morphed as they absorbed bits and pieces from the others, and incorporated those beliefs and practices into their own paths.

Within the last sixty years, the world has seen a new revitalization of the Ancient Gods and Goddesses, with a rising population of people bowing and praying to Isis, Baphomet, Set, Sekmet, Athena, Zeus, Hera, Odin, Gwydion, Adroa, Nyambi, Evaki and many other Gods and Goddesses of our globe's past.

Today's Witches practice ceremonies that resemble those performed by ancient Americans, Egyptians, Romans, and the Norse, among others. Witches today summon the aid of spirits, resembling methods used by Native Americans and Sumerians, both wildly different cultures, but with similar beliefs about the dead. Witches today practice healing techniques with plants, the same way Druids, Natives, and others have. Witches today, more so than others, acknowledge the possibility of sixth senses, such as ESP (Extra-Sensory Perception) and phenomena like OBE (Out of Body Experience). Some Witches also throw curses around when agitated, although this isn't acceptable within Wicca, where morality is supreme, and a lack of it has consequences.

Witchcraft today is the product of evolution in progress, gaining in prominence and strength. With every generation, we learn more healing techniques, ceremonies, rites, spells, incantations, and methods of Magic. People can now perform Magic using components that might not have been previously available to them, making religious exploration more assessable to more people.

As with Witchcraft, Modern Wicca also contains cultural influences from a variety of sources, depending on the location of the practitioners. American Wicca is every bit as culturally inclusive as American Witchcraft, but Wicca has more clearly defined roots, planted deeply in Europe.

Most folks credit England's Gerald Gardner as being the Father of modern Wicca, and the only people I've heard dispute this are ceremonial magicians and students of Aleister Crowley.

A dear friend, Augustus Numley, being one of these, insists that Crowley is the father of modern Witchcraft, and therefore the father of Wicca, or at the very least, a grandfather. I argue that, while Crowley is certainly relevant, he's more of a *great-uncle*. I do believe that Crowley influenced Gardner, but I'm more tempted to argue that Wicca was a rejection of Crowley's hedonistic philosophies, rather than a distorted copy. Crowley's popular phrase, *"Do what they wilt, shall be the whole of the law,"* while similar to the Wiccan phrase, *"An' harm ye none, do as you will"* - they have vastly different meanings and express two distinctly different Magical philosophies and lifestyles.

Wicca's creed, *An harm ye none, do as you will*, is more aligned with the teachings of Christ or Buddha, than Crowley, so while Gardner may have absorbed bits and pieces of many previous philosophers, including Crowley and others, the Wiccan religion that Gardner fathered is vastly different where it counts, *morality,* and that morality is ultimately what distinguishes Wiccans from other Witches.

Moral codes might differ slightly between Wiccan covens, but the core philosophy of *not harming others* usually provides the base for all of them. Many Wiccans prohibit magic performed on someone without their knowledge, except for healing prayers, spells, and rituals. Most Wiccans do no perform any sort of manipulative Magic on others, which seeks to alter one's will, without their knowledge or consent. *Curses* are normally out of the question and aren't aligned with Wiccan philosophies. *Love Spells* can be tricky, but do-able within the confines of Wicca, but you must take heed not to target love spells toward an unknowing or unwilling person. Instead, you might aim your magical workings and daily actions toward sending love out into the world. If you send love out, it'll boomerang back at triple potency, known as the Three-Fold Law.

Hans Baldung Grien, Witches Brewing, Strassburg, 1514. Picture provided by Dover Publications, courtesy of Ernst & Johanna Lehner, from their book, Devils Demons & Witchcraft, 1971.

Three-Fold Law

The Three-Fold Law, mentioned in Wiccan Rede, is a belief that one's magic, whether good or bad, will come back to them with three-times the potency. Other students of Witchcraft or Mysticism paths might believe the rule extends to six or even nine times, while some reject the theory altogether. Wiccans for the most part, believe that whatever you send out into the world, you'll get back, times three. To see this in action, let's say you curse someone because they ran over your cat. According to the rule of three, you'd receive that curse back, or some form of negativity, but three-times worse. On the inverse, if you perform a healing prayer on someone, you'd receive that blessing, or some form of positivity, but three-times better.

Gods & Goddesses

Since I began my studies into various religions over twenty years ago, and especially as the owner of a metaphysical business, I've learned that dang near everyone in the Pagan community bows down to a different deity. And, that's just fine. While most Covens will agree as a group on issues such as deity names and idols, a solitary practitioner may pray to whatever deity he or she chooses. For this reason, I've written this book to be versatile, for anyone to use, regardless of their particular preferences in deities.

Simply incorporate your chosen God/s or Goddesses into the spells and rituals when necessary. This will also help personalize the spells for you, which some feel encourages the effectiveness of the work you're performing. While most Wiccans bow down to both a God & Goddess, I've seen some focus on one over the other, but be warned: a coven that focuses only on the Goddess and not the God, or the God and not the Goddess, isn't truly in line with the traditional Wiccan path. I've seen covens do it, and claim themselves Wiccan as they do it, but traditional Wiccan revere both the male and female aspects of nature, humanity, and deities. So, if you want to stay true to the Wiccan way, it would be proper to pick two deities representing male and female aspects.

Some Wiccans believe in a higher being or entity, above that of the God and Goddess. This isn't uncommon. This entity represents the unknown forces within the universe, easily comparable to the Christian concept of Jehovah or the Jewish concept of Yahweh, or even Ancient Egyptian's Akhenaten's reverence of Aten. In each of these cases, there's a supreme being, above that of Gods and Goddesses. The Gods and Goddesses represent aspects of that force. Male-female, love-war, creation-destruction, etc. The chart on the next page gives examples from various cultures, to illustrate the similarities between religions.

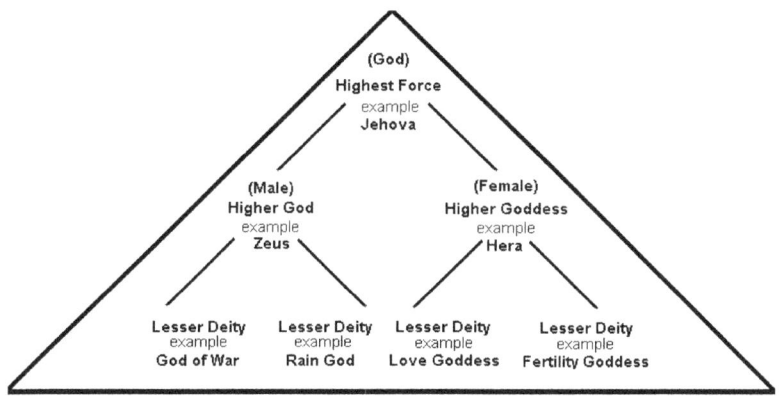

What Makes Successful Magic

What makes Magic work? There are various factors at play which lead to successful magic, some with a bit of scientific backing - with regard to the medicinal properties of plants, and psychological factors at play during worship, prayers, and spell-crafting. While Witches, Shamans, and healers used plants in their practices for thousands of years, our modern-day researchers are now looking into the various properties, some with surprisingly similar results to those of previously reported by Witches, Shamans, and healers. Studies have shown that aromatherapy is not a web of wives' tales as some previously thought. As you collect spells, prayers, chants, and other bits for your personal book of shadows, I'd also encourage you to keep an eye open for new herbal research studies and incorporate their findings into your own book of shadows.

The healing qualities of herbs and plants can be obtained in many ways and will vary per situation. Some herbs are taken internally, some are applied externally, some are burned as incense, etc. If the herb is to be taken internally, the safest and most accurate method would be to purchase a bottle of pharmaceutical grade supplement and follow the directions. Using dried herbs from a reputable herb dealer are great, too, but dosing can become an issue if there are variables with the potency. As with any herb you use, I can't emphasize the importance of researching any and all herbs before you use them, and keep an eye on those research studies.

The most important thing you can do, is to believe in yourself as a source of Magic. Until a person realizes that they have the potential to make powerful changes, they will be unsuccessful at their efforts. Self-esteem, faith, and will-power makes a difference in one's abilities, and what you *believe* you can do, will impact what you *do*.

Page from Egyptian Book of Dead. Picture provided by Dover Publications, courtesy of Ernst & Johanna Lehner, from their book, Devils Demons & Witchcraft, 1971.

Initiation into Wicca

The Initiation act serves as a mental and physical acknowledgment of walking the Wiccan path. It's also a cleansing act, similar to a Christian Baptism. The initiation is a rebirth of your spiritual senses, and an awakening of your consciousness, and more specifically a declaration to yourself and the God & Goddess that you are adopting a new positive lifestyle and mindset from that point forward. It marks a point in time when you made a choice to be Wiccan, and walk a fair and righteous path, and uphold the values expressed in the Wiccan Rede.

Coven Initiations

If you're seeking initiation into a Coven, you should examine your motives - and theirs, before making a commitment to be a part of the group. There's a few things you might consider beforehand, and you need to make sure you and the group are morally aligned with each other. The coven you join should reflect your beliefs about Magic and they should never force you to compromise your values or morals. They should not ask for money beyond ten percent of an income, which is the industry standard among most Christian and Jewish congregations, too. If you find that the coven's money isn't getting spent toward the betterment of the group, consider a different group. The position of High Priest or Priestess can attract people who enjoy leadership - too much. As with *any* religion, there's a chance that some spiritual leader's motives aren't going to be pure, and it's important for you to recognize when things aren't on the up and up. Plainly put, you need to be able to recognize a potential cult.

Be cautious and gauge any prospective groups for abhorrent moralities, sexually deviant behaviors, or any other activities that might make you feel uncomfortable. Sadly, occult or Witchcraft related cults do occur, but thankfully- aren't the norm. If a group insists on being naked during ceremonies, and you aren't okay with that, don't allow yourself to be forced into practicing naked. It's not a Wiccan thing…except to nudist-Wiccans. I'm not judging, I'm just saying, you don't have to get naked, and there are plenty of covens out there that aren't based upon a nudist philosophy.

Orgies and altar-sex are also *not* a part of modern Wicca, and if you find a coven of screw-anything Wiccans, you should know that isn't normal. Never let a coven pressure, insist, or even casually mention that you need to sexually engage with people for Wiccan purposes. Sexual harassment or assault in a coven is no different than the workplace, or the parking lot of your grocery store. I'd like to make *that* crystal clear.

If a priest/priestess approach you with sexual advances or suggestions that you perform nude or sexually, it's important for you to understand that they're full of shit, and they're using their position for sexual gratification…and you should plan an exit strategy, because *that* my friend, is a cult.

Your coven needs to be a group of people you feel safe with, above all else. They need to be looking out for your best interests, with concern for your general well-being. If a group isn't doing that, they aren't worth being a part of. If a priest or priestess constantly degrades or humiliates you or other coven members, or forces people to perform questionable acts, run. That's not what a coven is about, my friend, and you've gotten mixed up with the wrong folks.

Most Wiccan covens are awesome and filled with some of the most beautiful souls this planet offers, but occasionally there's an asshole in the mix, and it's important that you recognize what's real Wicca, and what's not. An orgy is an orgy regardless if it's with Wiccans, Satanists, Furries, or Southern Baptists. Orgies are not a Wiccan thing…except to sexually promiscuous-Wiccans. Orgies spread herpes and gonorrhea, not love. They are dangerous, and they aren't a part of modern Wicca, at least not in *my* book.

I'm not hating on sexual oriented Magic, either. I've included a few sexually natured spells within *this* book. Certainly, sex Magic has a place between consenting adults, but not within *Wiccan covens*, and certainly not under *coercion*.

If promiscuity and exhibitionism appeal to you, you'll likely feel more at home with Satanists, or maybe with Witches who practice Magic from a *different* branch of the Witchcraft tree, one specifically devoted to sexually geared ceremonial Magic. Again, no judgements, but there is a clear necessity to define these boundaries within in Modern Wicca for the safety of our practitioners against predators.

Self-Initiations

There are many Wiccan initiation rites and ceremonies out there, and one isn't necessarily better than another, but the absolute easiest and most appropriate self-initiation would be to recite the Wiccan Rede…and *mean it*. Some ceremonies can be as complex as formal weddings, or as simple as an unspoken vow between you and the higher powers. Do what you feel comfortable with. If you're searching for a simple cleansing / self-initiation ceremony, I've included one below. Feel free to change the text as needed, as it's the *intent* that's important, not the wording.

Simple Self-Initiation Rite

Begin by lighting frankincense, rosemary, or cedar incense. Any scent will work, but these three are popular cleansing scents. Let the incense burn for a few minutes while you prepare yourself a warm bath of clear water, free of soap, salts, oils, or herbs.

Slip into the bath and visualize the water cleansing away all of your doubts, hostilities, agitations, and stress. Concentrate on the water rinsing away negativity and cleansing your body, spirit and mind of any obstacles that prevent peace. Once your thoughts are clear, reflect on what the Wiccan path represents. Consider the words behind the Wiccan Rede, and how you can use them to be a better person. What are your plans as you journey along the Wiccan path? How can you bring more positivity into the world through Wicca?

When you feel ready, you may recite the below passage silently or aloud.

Bless me, God and Goddess, as I cleanse myself of all negativity, past, present, and future. Protect me, God and Goddess, as I commence my walk along the Wiccan path.

I vow to do good, as is the Wiccan Way. I vow to be good, as is the Wiccan Way. I vow to promote goodness in others through my own actions. I vow to speak with kindness and respect for others, whether deserved or not. Guide me, God and Goddess, as I work magically, spiritually, and physically for the betterment of others and myself. Grant me favor as I work to bring your love and light into being for myself and all.

With your Blessings, God & Goddess, So mote it be.

When you've finished reciting the above passage, you may get out of the water and dry your Wiccan-self off!

Personal Notations

Chapter 2
Spell Components & Tools

Tools

You'll find the tools and components described in this book are simple and most are easy to obtain. They're kept to a minimum for easy and targeted magic, including candles, oils, incenses, sachets, poppet dolls, pendulums, rune stones, and other common devices within modern Wicca.

Candles

Candles are probably the most widely used tool in Wicca, as they provide a perfect medium for performing simple, effective, and relatively inexpensive Magic. Candles can promote various properties, depending on the color of the candle, oils used to anoint them, and the herbs used to scent them. You can anoint a candle with oils by rubbing them oil onto the candle as you concentrate on the desired effect of the spell.

Multi-Colored Candles

Multi colored candles are used for adding multiple attributes to your candle Magic. For example, let's say you're using a blue candle to perform a healing spell. To add power to the spell, you could use a Black and Blue candle. The Black would represent the power, while the Blue would represent the healing. You could also use a Red & Blue candle for the healing spell. Red would represent the passion to heal.

Multi colored candles are also used in many various sects of Wicca to represent both the God and Goddess united. The Black sometimes representing the God, with the white representing the Goddess. Black and White candles are also used to represent both the good and evil forces you may be working with, similar to the Yin Yang concept of acknowledging opposites while attempting to create a balance. They can also be burned

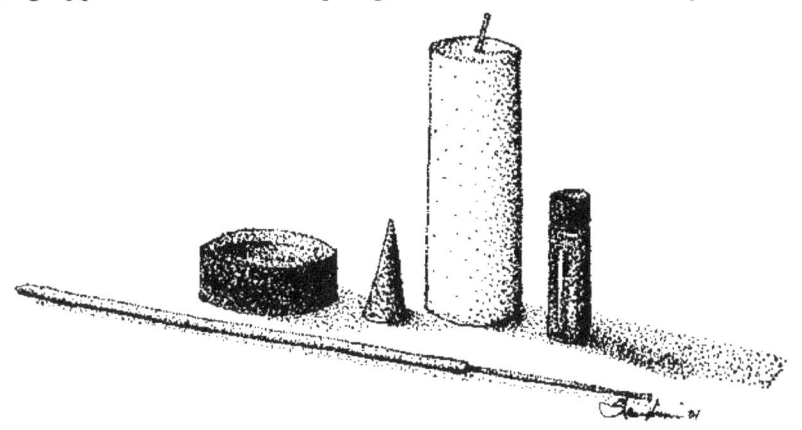

Tools, by Shawna Bowman, 2001

during purifications and cleansings, which is an attribute of the White candles, and the Black would add power your work.

Candle Magic can be as simple as lighting the candle and concentrating on the purpose it serves. Many Wiccans might first anoint their candles with oils. The oils you might use will differ, depending on the outcome desired. For example, Dragon's Blood Oil is used to strengthen spells. Remember the blue and black candle for healing I mentioned earlier? You could anoint it with Dragon's Blood Oil before burning for added potency.

Oils are considerably more expensive than dried or fresh herbs, and some are difficult to find, and so some prefer to anoint candles with infusions made fresh or dried herbs. An anointing infusion can be made using most any dried or fresh herb by letting it steep in hot water for about fifteen minutes. Generally, one teaspoon of herbs per cup of water will do the trick. After steeping, strain out the herbs and you're left with the anointing infusion. Take care to let it cool sufficiently before applying it candles.

As you anoint candles, it's important that you concentrate on the desired effect. If you're anointing a healing candle for someone with a cold, you might rub Rosemary onto a blue candle, and concentrate on their cold disappearing. Visualize the healing that will take place, and then visualize the person healed, without a cold.

Once the candle is anointed, some might sprinkle dried or fresh herbs into the pool of wax at the top as it burns to further enhance both the aroma and potency. If you add herbs to a candle, do not let it burn unattended. Take care to watch the candle closely as the herbs may periodically ignite.

Candle Dressing, by Shawna Bowman, 2001.

Magic with Colors

Below, you'll find the most common attributes associated with each color, this information will prove useful as you work toward creating your own spells in the future. Colored candle Magic is a super simple easy way to dabble with spell crafting.

White is most associated with cleansing, purity, protection, and represents the Goddess for many Wiccans.

Red is used in matters dealing with strong emotions, such as love, and anger. For this reason it is often used in revenge, or passion based spells.

Blue is generally used in matters pertaining to the promotion of health, and the recovery of illnesses, or ailments. It also is used when one wants to embody trust, and empathy in the eyes of others.

Yellow is usually used in magic dealing with new beginnings, or peaceful changes. Yellow is also burned to promote spiritual growth or positive changes.

Green is mostly associated with fertility and money, but is often used in healing spells. Its attributes might vary between practitioners and/or covens.

Black is used to add a little extra power to Wiccan practices. Black also embodies forceful attributes and might help in matters which require immediate attention and resolution. Within Wicca, black candles can be used to represent God on the alter, normally accompanied by a white candle representing the Goddess.

Purple is generally used when one is trying to obtain peace or tranquility. Purple will help promote a relaxing environment.
They too are commonly used in healing spells.

White is used primarily for cleansings, and protection. When you perform healing spells, white candles will certainly not hurt. You can also use them when working other general magic, for they represent the Goddess.

Pink is used for matters dealing with romance, desire, sex, fertility, and promoting peace in families.

Herbs

Herbs are a Witch's best friend, regardless of the path they follow, and their uses are limitless. Herbs are used in spell crafting, teas, baths, candles, oils, sachets, poppet dolls, cooking, brewing, etc. You're likely familiar with most of the herbs used within these pages, as I sincerely tried to keep you clear of any wild goose chases. Most of the herbs can be purchased through your local grocer, and the others can be easily found online. I urge you to **use caution** before using any herb internally or externally, and to **speak first with your doctor** about possible side effects, or risks of interactions with medications you take. **If you're pregnant or nursing, do not take in, or apply to your body, *any herb* without first consulting a doctor.** Children are at greater risk to suffer from adverse reactions from internally taken or externally applied herbs, and so you should **NEVER give your child any herbal concoction or external application** without first speaking with your doctor. Children's sensitive skins are susceptible to allergic reactions, especially from oils, so **DO NOT use oils in any fashion on infants, toddlers, or small children**. Nursing mothers should take caution, too, and not use oils on themselves while breast feeding, to avoid adverse reactions on the baby's super-sensitive skin.

I'd be careful of substitutions and wildcrafted herbs. If you plan on picking your own herbs, make sure to have a reputable herb identification guide handy. In Texas, my go-to guy for all things herb related is a man known as Merriwether, a notable foraging teacher, botanist, chemist, and survival expert. He presents accurate information and recipes, while explaining the science behind their uses and their effectiveness. You can check out his Facebook page: Merriwether's Foraging Texas. For those not in Texas, I promise his page will still be helpful to anyone in the United States. If you hunt up an herbalist in your specific area, make sure to find one whose methods are rooted in science, especially for identifying herbs you plan on eating or drinking. You need to make absolute certain you're getting the right herb, and for that you should have experts in your corner. Wikipedia and Merriwether's resources used together can tell you a great deal about many of the herbs you might work with.

Found below are the herbs, fruits, and plant products you'll run across as you read through the spells. You're probably familiar with most of them. I encourage you to research any that are unfamiliar to you, particularly if ingested. The scientific names presented represent the species used commercially and medicinally and considered safe for use as described within this book. Some herbs, such as rose, mint, lavender, echinacea will have many other varieties to choose from. If you go with another species, do your research to make sure the species is safe and the medicinal qualities match those of the recommended species.

Almonds *(Prunus amygdalus)*
Apple *(Malus pumila)*
Basil *(Ocimum basilicum)*
Chamomile *(Chamaemelum nobile)*
Cinnamon *(Cinnamomum verum)*
Clove *(Syzygium aromaticum)*
Comfrey *(Symphytum officinale)*
Damiana *(Turnera diffusa)*
Dragon's Blood *(Daemonorops draco)*
Echinacea *(Echinacea angustifolia)*
Eucalyptus *(Eucalyptus globulus)*
Fenugreek *(Trigonella foenum-graecum)*
Frankincense *(Boswellia sacra)*
Garlic *(Allium sativum)*
Ginger *(Zingiber officinale)*
Honeysuckle *(Lonicera caerulea or japonica)*
Lavender *(Lavandula angustifolia or latifolia)*
Mint *(Mentha piperita or spicata)*
Mugwort *(Artemisia vulgaris)*
Myrrh *(Commiphora myrrha)*
Passion Flower (*Passiflora incarnata*)
Patchouli (*Pogostemon cablin*)
Rose (*Rosa damascene, or centifolia*)
Rosemary (*Rosmarinus officinalis*)
St. John's Wort (*Hypericum perforatum*)
Valerian (*Valeriana officinalis*)
Sage (*Salvia officinalis*)
Sandalwood (*Santalum spicatum*)

Sachets

Sachets are herbs placed in a pouch or small bag. You can make a sachet by using small bits of old material or cloth and tying the herbs with string or yarn inside of the cloth. Sachets are usually placed in a particular spot or carried with you for the desired effect. The color of the fabric should embody the purpose of the sachet, for example, a healing sachet might be blue, white, or purple. A money sachet could be black or green, and so forth. Refer to the previously mentioned section on colors to give your sachets a color boost for the herbs inside.

Sachets, by Shawna Bowman, 2001

Oils

Below, you'll find a list of oils mentioned in the spells to come. I recommend using fresh, high-quality oils in your magical practices, whether for healing or not. Good oils will stay fresh and usable longer. Cheap oils tend to turn bad quicker.

Cedar *(Juniperus ashei or J. deppeana)*
Cinnamon *(Cinnamomum verum)*
Clove *(Syzygium aromaticum)*
Dragon's Blood *(Daemonorops draco)*
Eucalyptus *(Eucalyptus globulus)*
Frankincense *(Boswellia sacra)*
Honeysuckle (*Lonicera caerulea or japanica*)
Lavender *(Lavandula angustifolia or latifolia)*
Mint *(Mentha piperita or spicata*
Myrrh *(Commiphora myrrha)*
Patchouli *(Pogostemon cablin)*
Rose (*Rosa damascene, or R. centifolia*)
Rosemary *(Rosmarinus officinalis)*
Sage *(Salvia officinalis)*
Sandalwood (*Santalum spicatum*)
Sweet Almond Oil *(Prunus amygdalus)*
Tea Tree *(Melaleuca alternifolia)*

Incenses

Most of the spells within this collection will involve some form of incense. There are many kinds in all shapes and sizes, but the most popular and readily available are sticks, cones, and charcoal incense. If you can't find the particular scent needed, feel free to make substitutions with herbs that share similar properties.

Below are most of the common scents you will be using.

Chamomile *(Chamaemelum nobile)*
Cedar *(Juniperus ashei or J. deppeana)*
Cinnamon *(Cinnamomum verum)*
Clove *(Syzygium aromaticum)*
Dragon's Blood *(Daemonorops draco)*
Eucalyptus *(Eucalyptus globulus)*
Frankincense *(Boswellia sacra)*
Honeysuckle (*Lonicera caerulea or japanica*)
Lavender *(Lavandula angustifolia or latifolia)*
Mint *(Mentha piperita or spicata)*
Myrrh *(Commiphora myrrha)*
Patchouli *(Pogostemon cablin)*
Rose (*Rosa damascene, or R. centifolia*)
Rosemary *(Rosmarinus officinalis)*
Sage *(Salvia officinalis)*
Sandalwood (*Santalum spicatum*)

Charcoal Burner, by Shawna Bowman, 2001.

Stones

Many Wiccans utilize stones in their spell crafting. I've presented the most common of these stones for you, below, along with their attributes.

Agate is said to bring strength to the mind and body. It's also worn for courage, and is believed to promote healing, and peacefulness.

Amber is a yellowish-brown stone from fossilized tree resin, and is used for balancing, harmonizing, and promoting general well-being. It's also used to dispel negativity.

Amethyst, a lavender to purple variety of quartz, is said to strengthen the immune system. It's also used to aid with combating mental disorders and addiction. Amethyst is also said to increase psychic and channeling abilities, as well as general intelligence.

Bloodstone is beautiful dark green stone with maroon veins. It's said to be a great healing stone, perfect for diseases of the heart, spleen, and the liver in particular. Others use it for its abilities to promote the reduction of stress. It too is believed to increase psychic abilities.

Copper is used to aid with the flow of blood, increase metabolism, increase energy, and create mental stability.

Diamonds are used predominately to promote faithfulness but are also used to increase brain function. They are also believed to promote purity, and to dispel negativity.

Emeralds are said to strengthen the nervous system. They are also believed to enhance meditation, dreams, and psychic awareness.

Garnets are believed to revitalize the entire body, and are said to promote love, kindness, and peace.

Gold is said to draw in positive energy to your aura, and to speed up tissue repair and regeneration.

Hematite, an elegant, iridescent-like metallic black stone, has been used for thousands of years, and continues to be a prominent stone in Magic shops today. The most common use is for protection, but other popular uses are for strength, and courage. It's believed that if you are partial to Hematite, and like the appearance and color of the stone, the stone will work its Magic better for you than others who are impartial.

Jade is often used to dispel negativity, and to impart wisdom and insight. It is also commonly used in money spells and is to be carried with you for good luck in your financial matters.

Jasper is believed to be a very potent general healing stone, used for a variety of ailments and illnesses.

Lapis Lazuli is one of my favorite stones, for its deep rich blue color. The stone is usually veined with gold, which made it a favorite of the Ancient Egyptians, who used it to adorn everything from sarcophagus, tapestries, statues, necklaces and anything they wanted to look regal. Today, it's used to increase psychic abilities, and to aid in obtaining contact with higher beings and spirits.

Moonstone, another one of my favorites, is identified by its milky white appearance. It's used as a general healing stone and also to aid in psychic communications. It's also used for healing female issues and is said to create emotional balance and stability.

Obsidian, a beautiful black stone, is said to help clear the mind of obstacles while meditating and contacting spirits. It's also used for general healing when carried as an amulet.

Onyx is used to help aid in relieving stress, and encourages balance. It is also said to help maintain emotional balance and help control bad tempers.

Opal is said to increase the relationship between you and God, strengthening the connection. It's also been used to aid in balancing emotions. Some with streaks of multi-colored shimmering crystals.

Quartz crystal is the most common stone used in Wicca. The uses for crystals range from spirit summoning to healing pain, from dispelling negativity to providing protection. It's been said that whenever you tote a crystal with you, it will give you energy when you need it, and store it when you produce too much, almost like an energy regulator. Crystals are also used for meditation, to clear the mind and body of external vibrations.

Rose Quartz's soft pink hue is often a slightly translucent, but milky color. Rose Quartz today is most used in Love Spells, but still maintains a strong presence in healing techniques. It has been used for healing headaches, if placed underneath the pillow while napping. It's also reported to relieve stress, emotional imbalances. It is also supposed to bring about feelings of peace, and tranquility in an environment where it is placed.

Tiger's Eyes is another beautiful stone still being utilized. It's a yellow and brown striped stone, used to dispel negativity and also for obtaining truth or clarity on an issue.

Turquoise is another stone used for aiding in meditation and is also believed to increase creativity in whoever possesses it. Its most popular use is wearing or carrying it for protection.

Blessed Water

Blessed Water serves the same function and is made the same way as Holy Water. The uses for Blessed Water are many, and it remains to this day a valuable tool in almost every religion. Voodoo shops might call it Devil Water, some call it Blessed Mother Mary Water, but it's ultimately all the same, which is water that's been blessed through a prayer or ritual.

Wiccans and other Witches use Blessed Water in their Magical workings, primarily for cleansings and protection. Its purposes are unlimited, though, and some use it during healing Magic, some using for removing spirits, some for purifications, and non-Wiccans might use it conjunction with banishings and curses.

Producing Blessed Water needs to be done when your spiritual attunement, and/or awareness is high, and you are comfortable and confident about performing Magic. You need to be in a content frame of mind. From there, Blessing water can be as simple as a prayer, which I'll include below, or more ritualistic, which I'll also include further below.

To Bless your water in the simplest fashion, gather up natural water, either from a lake, ocean, creek, pond, puddle, etc. If you're going to store the water for later use, you can sterilize it by boiling it for several minutes, then allowing it to cool before performing the Blessing.

Blessed Water Prayer

My Lord and Lady, my God and Goddess, I ask that you grant your Blessings upon this gathered water, so that I may use it in your names to protect, purify, and to heal. May it protect the land on which it's spread. May it heal those whose skin it touches. May it bring love and light, with peace and tranquility to those in need. I promise, Lord and Lady, to use it wisely, and to honor your names as I work. So mote it be.

Ceremonial Water Blessing

For those desiring a little more ceremony, the Ceremonial Blessing might be more to your liking. You can set up your area, as shown in the drawing found below. There's no need to have a physical circle drawn, with salt or string, or anything else. I personally don't perform an opening and closing of the circle in my Magic, as some do, but if it's something you're interested in incorporating into your Magic, you can Google several methods by others online.

I use white candles all the way around for this, but you can use whatever colors you'd like. I also recommend that you use Frankincense, if available, but any scent will work.

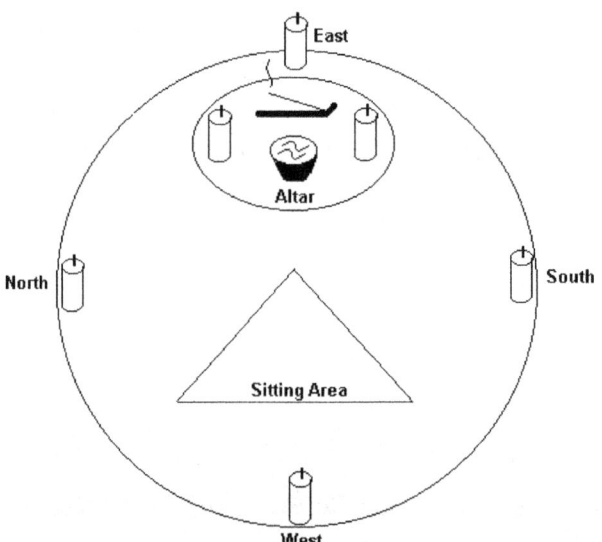

Begin by lighting each of the candles and the incense. Kneel or sit in front of the bowl of water. Concentrate on connecting with the God and Goddess. When you feel ready, repeat the Blessed Water Prayer, found on the previous page. After the prayer, extinguish the incense and candles, and you can store the Blessed Water for future use.

Healing Poppet Dolls

The Healing Poppet is the Wiccan name ascribed to dolls used in Magic, similar to Voodoo Dolls, though the two differ *greatly* in how they're used. While similar in concept, Wiccans only use the dolls for healing or positive purposes. The origins of these effigy dolls are said by some to originate with the cunning folk in Britain. If you look at the entry on Wikipedia for Voodoo Dolls and Poppet Dolls, they say the same things, even boldly stating for the latter that, "It was from these European dolls {of the cunning folk} that the myth of voodoo dolls arose." The truth is, effigy dolls are *much older* than either Poppets or Voodoo dolls, and they've been used in some Magical capacity by almost every culture on the planet since the dawning of man, with the oldest being a German artifact, Venus of Hohle Fels, dated to be around 40,000 years old. Another, the Venus of Willendorf, found in Austria is around 25,000 years old. Other ancient cultures in Britain, Africa, Japan, Russia, and North America, among others, created similar dolls to serve as protective objects, fertility charms, and to represent their revered deities. The first dolls within each of these cultures were likely made from mud and sticks, fashioned together with botanical matter, with stone, pottery, and cloth dolls to follow as humanity progressed and our tools improved.

For our purposes, the dolls themselves can be made from any pattern or design, from any material, though it's worth mentioning that some believe using an article of clothing from whomever the doll represents, will make the doll more effective. In fact, many believe *any* item belonging to the person represented would be ideal, for either the cloth or the stuffing, but it's not completely necessary. As long you perceive the doll to be a representation of the person, you're on the right track. Some people, not wishing to sew, might opt for purchasing a premade doll, but many believe it's the *work* you put into making the poppet doll, that encourages successful results. If you're looking for a shortcut, but still want to put the work in with an *easier* project, you can do as the ancients, and make a stick-doll by tying twigs together with a vine or twine. Again, as long as the doll symbolizes the person, even vaguely, as I said before, you're on the right track, and this includes literal stick figures.

The instructions that follow are for a standard modern stuffed poppet doll. It's a pretty easy sewing project using two pieces of fabric that are cut and sewn together, then lightly stuffed, and sewn shut. Any ailments that you'd like to target for healing may be stitched onto to the finished doll. With stick-dolls, you'd use twine or a vine to mark the areas of interest.

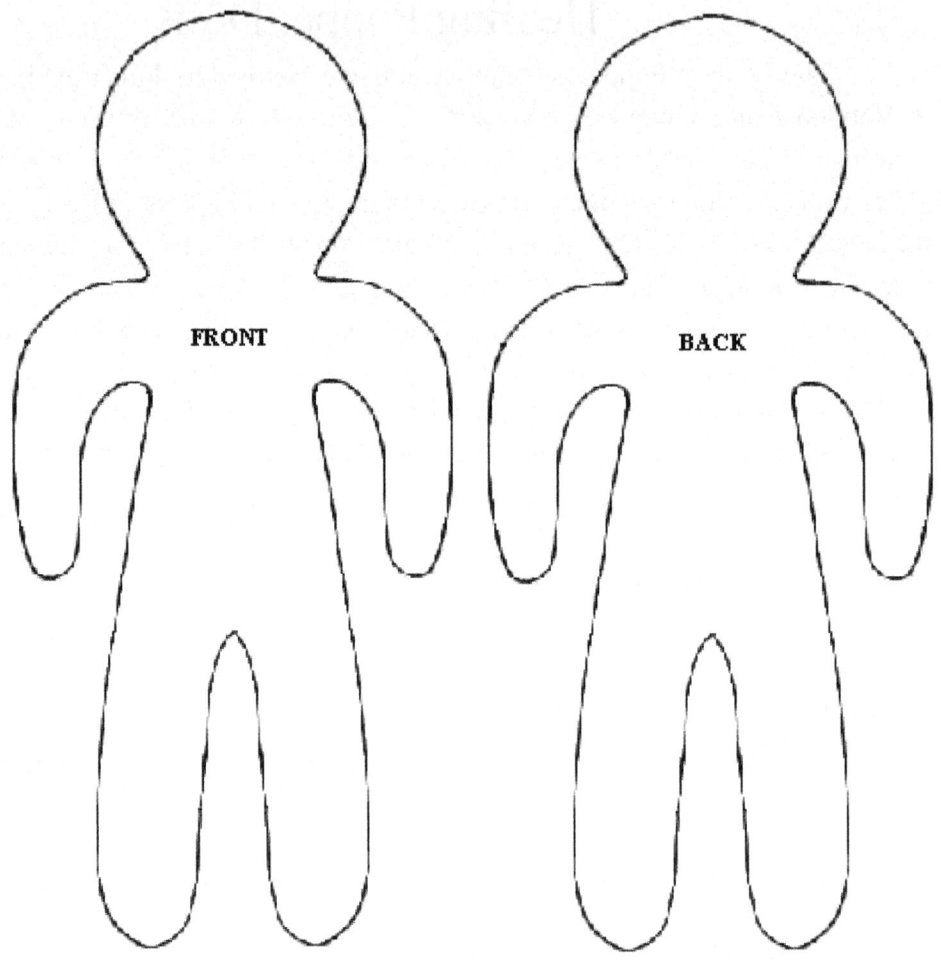

As you create your own pattern, keep in mind; you'll be hand-sewing the doll together, so you might want to keep the size of the doll fairly small, if time or skill is an issue. After you've drawn the front and back of the pattern, which might look like the sample above, you can cut them out, and place them together so they match up.

Begin sewing at the shoulder area and work your way down the body, then back up to the other shoulder, making sure to leave the head portion open. When sewing is complete, insert the stuffing through the head area. Fill the dolls with your choice of stuffing, which might include cotton, straw, herbs, articles of clothing, etc. For added potency, you might consider adding a stone or two with helpful healing attributes.

For the doll to be effective, most agree that you need to concentrate on healing the sick person as you make the doll. Try to limit outside distractions as much as possible while you create the doll to keep your concentration focused, and your intent clear as you work. Music is fine, but I'd turn off televisions or other video devices while you sew. Place the finished doll in a safe place, where it will not be seen or disturbed by others.

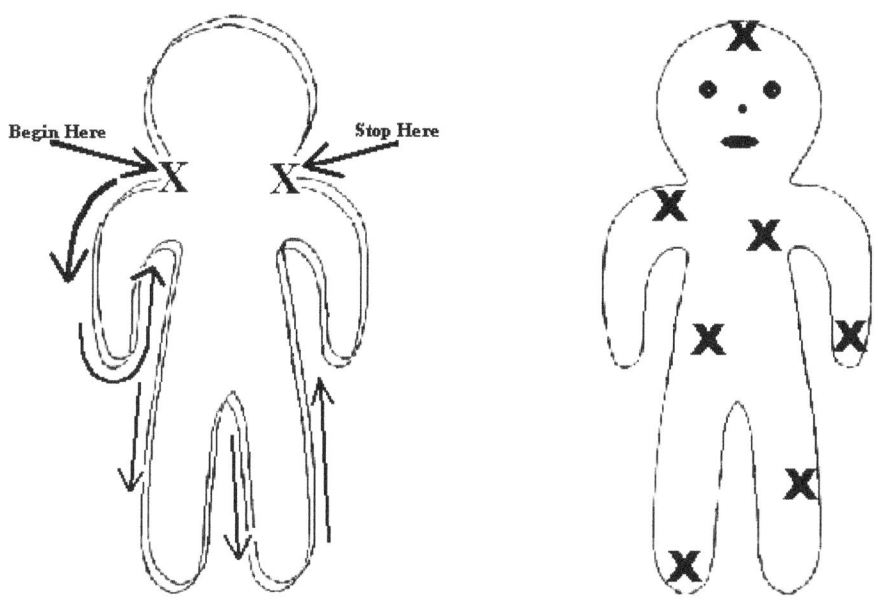

Talismans, Charms, Seals, & Amulets

The talismans, charms, & seals seen in this chapter are just a few of the various symbols used within Modern Wicca. The symbols are as varied as the Gods and Goddesses, but I've provided a few of the most common symbols and interpretations for you below.

An amulet is a natural talisman, usually found in the form of a rock with a hole in the center, also known as the witch's stone, or a wizard's rock, but amulets can also be carved stone with symbols or passages.

This is the basic pentagram, worn by most for it's protective properties. It has many various meanings, depending on what branch of Paganism you adhere to. The points of the star can represent parts of the body, elements, the directions, senses, and much more.

Pentacle

While the pentacle varies slightly in appearance to the pentagram, the uses are the same in most Pagan traditions.

The Pentagram as a Protective Seal

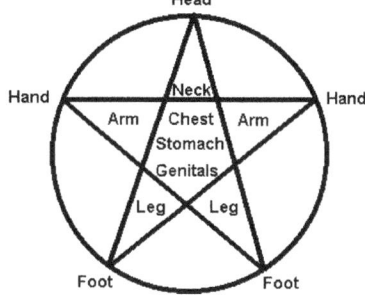

The Star itself serves to represent the human body, while the circle around it serves as protective sphere.

Elements of the Pentagram

Points of Direction Associated with Pentagrams & Pentacles

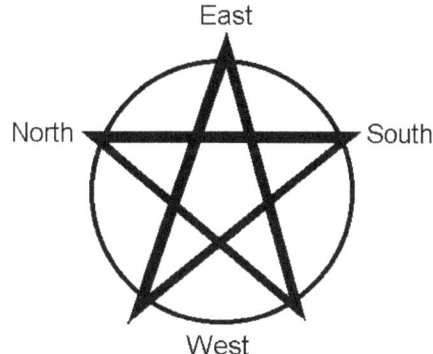

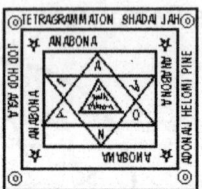

The talisman above, called The Almadel Seal, has been advertised as one of the most powerful seals, but can only be used for good. It is said to summon angels and helpful spirits for the purposes of healing and helping you. If you should wish to recreate this talisman, and use it for its Magical purposes, you should note that within the small triangle the text reads as follows:

HELL
HELION
ADONAIJ

It has also been recomended that this design be engraved onto silver or gold to be effective.

The Ancient Egyptian Ankh symbolizes eternal life. It is still used today by Wiccans, and other Pagans for its protective qualities.

Chapter 3
Times to Perform Magic

Holidays

Found below are the most commonly celebrated Wiccan holidays, though covens may have a few more or less, depending on the Gods and Goddesses and culture their coven reveres.

Candlemas
(Imbolc, Brigid)
February 2

Candlemas, or Imbolc, celebrates the anticipation and coming of spring. It is also a time for purification, and a great time for starting new projects. This is also a great time for starting your indoor seedlings for Spring planting.

Ostara
(Spring Equinox)
March 20-23 dates vary

The Spring Equinox is a celebration of the arrival of Spring. This is also a great time for fertility, cleansing, purification, initiations, and love spells. Traditionally, this signifies the start of the planting season, after the threat of a freeze has passed.

Beltane
(Walpurgis Night) April 30
(May Day) May 1

Beltane and May Day are both celebrations of beauty, and summer. Flowers and plants are always a great part of the festivities, as well as sweet refreshments. May Pole Dances are making a comeback, and if you've never been to one and participated, it's something you might enjoy. One of my fondest holiday memories are of a May Pole Dance and celebration in Nacogdoches, Texas during the 1990's. May Poles make a hugely entertaining events, and if you hear of one in your area, grab a long roll of ribbon and head to it! You won't regret it.

Litha
(Midsummer's Eve, Summer Solstice)
June 20-23 dates vary

The Summer Solstice celebrates the longest day of the year, with glory to the sun. Day Festivals are popular, with cool refreshments for the warm days.

Lughnassad
(Lammas)
August 1

Lammas is a celebration of the harvest. Traditionally, this would be one of the times of year for harvesting crops. Today, it is celebrated with appreciation toward the Earth in mind. The holiday spirit is shown by eating cakes, and other bread products such as cookies, and pies.

Mabon
(Fall Equinox)
September 20 - 30 date varies

The Fall Equinox is a wonderful celebration for the soon arrival of winter, and the end of summer. Traditionally, this would be the time for the second harvest for crops. Today, it celebrated with thankfulness for abundance in mind. At this time of year, be thankful for the abundance of food you have by celebrating with wine and savory pies.

The Tragicall Histoire of the Life & Death of Doctor Faustus, 1631. Picture provided by Dover Publications, courtesy of Ernst & Johanna Lehner, from their book, Devils Demons & Witchcraft, 1971.

Samhain
(Halloween, All Hallows Eve, November's Eve)
October 31

My personal favorite of the Pagan holidays, Halloween, is celebrated by many, regardless of one's religious identity. Traditionally, it represents the final harvest. All the crops are dying off, and what you have, is all you have, until spring. This could have been a grim time for some, in the "old days" if that last harvest wasn't good enough. This time of year, has subsequently been associated with death in many different cultures. Some choose to laugh death in the face, by dressing and facing the prospects of death head-on. Some believe this is an optimal time for making contact with the deceased.

Just a couple days after Halloween, Hispanic cultures celebrate Dia de los Muertos, or Day of the Dead, a day spent remembering and revering deceased ancestors, and paying tribute to their memories. Participants often paint their faces with skulls and wear beautiful suits and gowns, and taking to the streets to celebrate the fond memories of their loved ones with their friends and families, with food, drink, and merriment.

Yule
(Winter Solstice)
December 20 - 23 dates vary

Yule is the longest night of the year and celebrates Winter and the Horned God. This is a great time for a crisp celebration in the woods with a camp fire and friends. Staying warm with a Yule Log in the fireplace is also a great option, with a mug of warm spiced cider wine. Traditionally, this was a difficult time of year for some, as they were living off what remained from the final Fall harvest. Fresh vegetables are scarce, and hunting was harder, making for tough times. Yule allowed for a short splurge, and an opportunity to revere the Horned One, in the hopes that he'd help you make it through 'till Spring.

Albrecht Durer, Witch on goat to Walpurgisnacht, provided by Dover Publications, courtesy of Ernst & Johanna Lehner, from their book, Devils Demons & Witchcraft, 1971.

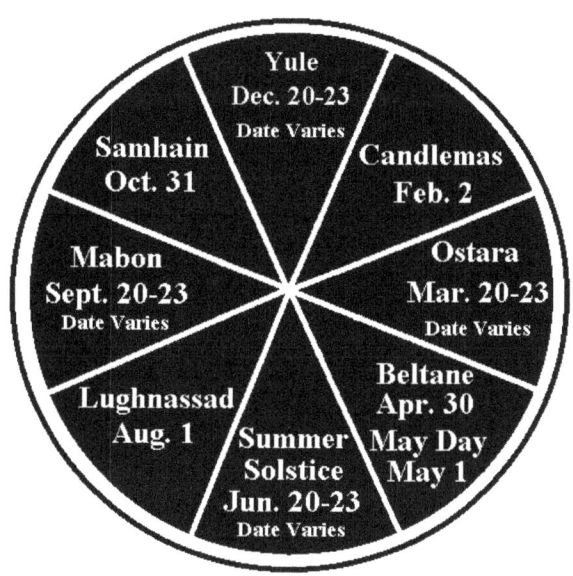

Winter Solstice

Feel his arrival in the brisk Yule winds,
See his coming in the steel gray skies,
In the barren oaks, with mistletoe hanging forth,

The Dark One awakes, with the birth of death.
The trees, dormant, hide his shadows.
The cold skies carry his spirit,
The warm earth opens up to his cold kiss.

God has come, The Solstice is here,
May we celebrate with warm wine,
May we laugh with true merriment,
And be glad he has found us again.

D. Flowers 1994

Moon Phases

Unless otherwise noted, the spells in this book don't *need* to be performed at any particular time of the day, or during a certain moon phase, *but* utilizing certain phases might be helpful with spell crafting. Below, you'll find a quick reference guide for the moon phases and their common names. On the following page you'll find their attributes and how the phases might prove useful in your Magical workings and even your garden, according to many.

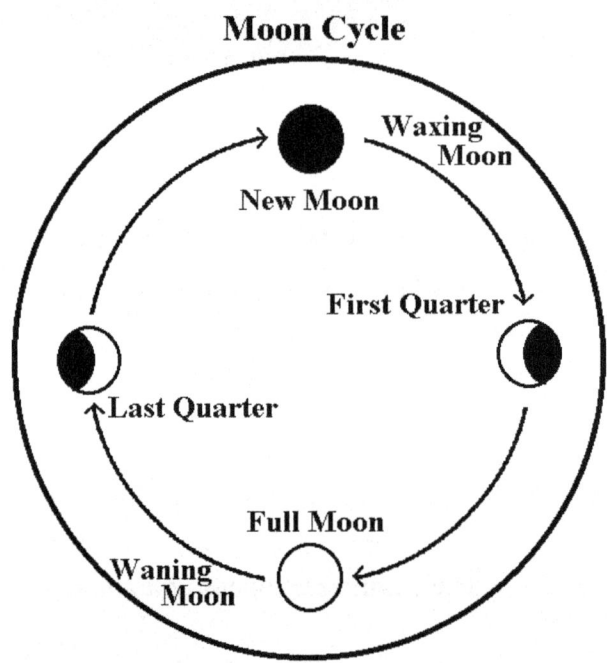

New Moon
(1st Quarter)
O

During the New Moon phase, the moon is not directly lit by sunlight. Many believe this a perfect time for divination. In the garden, this would be the perfect time to plant above land crops with outside seeds and flowering annuals.

Waxing Moon
(2nd Quarter)
(

During the Waxing phase, the moon is partially lit by the sunlight, but the light is increasing. Magically, this phase is a good time to perform prosperity, wealth, and fertility.

Full Moon
(3rd Quarter)
O

During the Full Moon phase, the moon is fully illuminated by the light of the sun. Magically, this phase is a great time for practicing Magic of all kinds. There is a high energy peak during the period before, during, and after a full moon, so use it wisely. This is also a great time for deep purification ceremonies. In the garden, now would be a good time to plant below ground crops, such as root crops, bulbous plants, biennials, and perennials.

Waning Moon
(4th Quarter)
)

During the Waning phase, the moon's light is decreasing. Magically, this would be an appropriate time to perform bindings, love spells, and Magic against others. Many consider this an inappropriate time for planting, instead it's a great time for mowing and weeding. Recurring growth will be slower if plants are cut or trimmed in this quarter.

Circle Magic

Some prefer performing their spells, prayers, and Magical workings within a *circle*. The circle itself can be imagined, or you can create a barrier with salt, string, or even tape. Whatever floats your boat here, will work. The altar area, too, may be imagined, but if you have an altar, certainly use it.

If you're not using an altar, simply place any spell or Magic components on the floor inside the (real or imagined) circle, as shown below. The bowls represent various herbs you might use during your spell crafting or Magical workings. As I noted during the Blessed Spell instructions, it's not required that you perform an opening or closing of the circle. In my own workings, I opt to begin my time in the circle by thanking the Gods & Goddesses for their help and guidance. When I've completed my work within the circle, I again express my gratitude and ask for their Blessings.

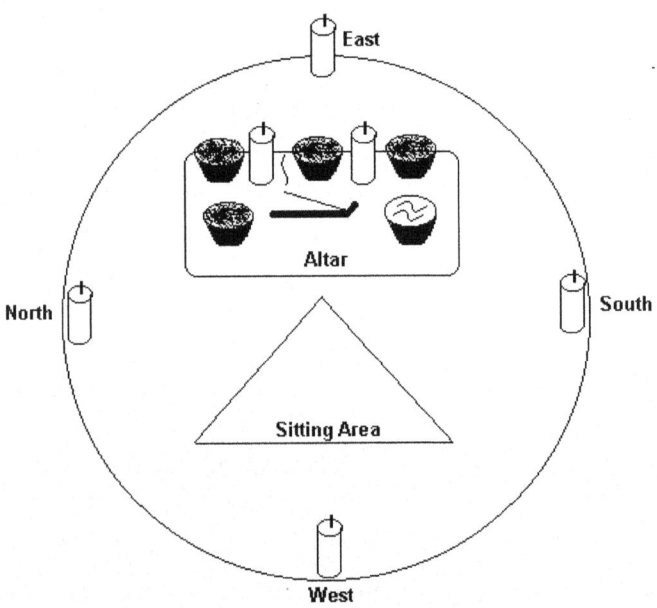

Part II Healing Spells

About the Spells
Cold & Flu
Pain Relief
Muscle Complaints
Female & Family Concerns
Insomnia
Skin Ailments
Stomach Ailments
Emotional Strain & Stress
Other Mentionable Healing Spells

About the Spells

We've come to the *Spells* portion of the book. Substitutions are not recommended when performing any of the healing spells, and as previously noted, I recommend that you research any herb you're working with, *before* you work with it. Some herbs, when digested may cause reactions when taken with other herbs or pharmaceuticals. If you're currently taking medications, check with your doctor or pharmacist before taking anything internally or applying anything externally. Pregnant or nursing women should avoid taking *any* and *all* herbs internally or externally, until they've checked first with their doctor.

Directly below, you'll find a sample of the spell format used throughout the remainder of the book.

Sample Spell

Line 1 - Targeted ailment or situation
Line 2 - {medium, mode, or means of magic}
Line 3 - # 101 Spell or Healing Method
Line 4 – Components: A list of the necessary ingredients needed for the spell.

Instructions for the spell will immediately follow the above information, as it is seen here. Line 1 (above) describes what the spell is targeting, and for what you are seeking assistance with. Line 2 describes the method or origins of the Magic technique. Line 3 illustrates the chronological spell or remedy number, as it's presented within the book. Line 4 lists your components needed for the spell or remedy.

Personal Notations

Chapter 4
Cold & Flu

Summer Cold
{Aromatherapy & Candle Magic}
1
Components: Eucalyptus Oil, White Candle

To help ease symptoms of a summer cold, gather together one white candle and a few drops of eucalyptus oil. Anoint the candle by rubbing it with a few drops of the oil, while concentrating on the desired effect. Light the candle and let it burn several minutes, until the wax at the top of the candle has melted into a small pool, then pour a few more drops of the oil into the melted wax. Keep the candle nearby as it burns, so that you can benefit from the scent as it permeates the room. If you enjoy the scent, feel free to burn the candle for as long as like.

Combat Fever
{Folk Remedy}
2
Components: Almonds

To help combat fevers, an old folk remedy indicates that you might eat almonds. Eating almost frequently is also believed by some to be a preventative measure against the onset of fevers.

Reduces Fever
{Aromatherapy & Candle Magic}
3
Components: Lavender Oil, Rosemary Oil & 1 Purple Candle

Gather together one purple candle, and Lavender & Rosemary oil. Anoint the candle by rubbing it with a few drops of the oils, while concentrating on the desired effect. Light the candle and let it burn several minutes, until the wax at the top of the candle has melted into a small pool, then pour a few more drops of the oils into the melted wax. Keep the candle nearby as it burns, so that you can benefit from the scent as it permeates the room. If you enjoy the scent, feel free to burn the candle for as long as like.

Keep away Fevers
{Folk Magic}
4
Components: Honeysuckle

An old Folk Magic method of keeping fevers at bay, is to grow Honeysuckle above your front door, and/or around the windows around your home.

Protection from Colds
{Aromatherapy & Folk Magic}
5
Components: Eucalyptus Leaves

Another method of preventing colds from taking hold, is to place fresh or dried eucalyptus leaves inside your pillowcase before going to sleep.

Cough Suppressant
{Aromatherapy}
6
Components: Eucalyptus Oil

To help suppress coughing, gather a few drops of eucalyptus oil and gently rub a few drops onto your chest area.

Ease Sore Throat
{Healing Gargle}
7
Components: Lavender Oil, Water

To help ease a sore throat, prepare a healing gargle. In an 8-ounce glass of water, place two drops of Lavender oil. Gargle with this mixture three times each in the morning and evening to help ease sore throats.

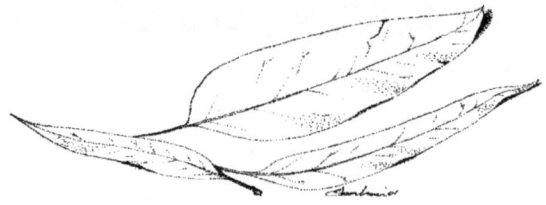

Eucalyptus Leaves, Shawna Bowman, 2001.

Colds and Coughs
{Folk Remedy}
8
Components: Garlic

Another method to help ease cold symptoms is to eat foods high in garlic. Eating garlic can also be used as a preventative measure during the cold and flu seasons.

Winter Blues
{Healing Bath & Tea}
9
Components: Dried Lavender Flowers and Dried St. John's Wort

To drive away winter blues, you might prepare yourself a Lavender bath, and a cup of St. John's Wort tea. Prepare the tea by gathering two teaspoons of dried St. John's Wort, and one cup boiling water. Remove the water from the heat, then add the herbs, and let it for at least ten minutes. Add sugar, honey, or other sweetener to adjust it to your liking.

For the Lavender bath, boil a few cups of water and remove it from the heat. Add a handful of dried Lavender flowers. Cover the pot and let it steep for about half an hour or longer. When the mixture has cooled, then strain out the spent herbs. Pour the strained lavender-water into a warm bath. Throw the used herbs outdoors or feed them to your houseplants or garden. If dried lavender flowers aren't available, simply add a few drops of lavender oil to your bath water.

With your tea brewed and your bath ready, slip into the bath. As you relax, become aware that you *can* control your mood. Concentrate on positive aspects of your life, and what you can do to help make positive improvements that might decrease symptoms of sadness. Try talking with a positive friend, listen to upbeat or uplifting music, or read books you enjoy. Change the focus of your attention and your mood with follow.

Note: Do not take St. John's Wort if you are taking *any* medications and avoid use with Valerian Root.

Bronchitis
{Aromatherapy & Candle Magic}
10
Components: Eucalyptus & Rosemary

To help fight bronchitis, gather together one blue candle, Eucalyptus oil, and Rosemary oil. Anoint the candle by rubbing it with a few drops each of the oils, while concentrating on the desired effect. Light the candle and let it burn several minutes, until the wax at the top of the candle has melted into a small pool, then pour a few more drops of the oils into the melted wax. Keep the candle nearby as it burns, so that you can benefit from the scent as it permeates the room. If you enjoy the scent, feel free to burn the candle for as long as like.

Eases Flu Symptoms
{Healing Bath}
11
Components: Dried Eucalyptus Leaves

To combat flu symptoms, prepare a Eucalyptus Bath. Gather a handful of dried and crushed Eucalyptus leaves and add them to several cups of boiling water. Remove it from the heat and let it step for at least ten minutes. After the mixture has cooled a bit, strain out the spent herbs. Pour the strained Eucalyptus water into a warm bath. Throw the used herbs outdoors or feed them to your houseplants or garden. If dried eucalyptus leaves aren't available, simply add a few drops of Eucalyptus oil to your bath water.

Relieve Nasal Congestion
{Healing Compress}
12
Components: Eucalyptus Leaves, Eucalyptus Oil, and 1 Rag or Cloth

To ease congestion, gather together a few drops of eucalyptus oil, a handful of dried, crushed eucalyptus leaves and several cups of water. Bring the water to a boil, then remove from the heat. Add the crushed, dried Eucalyptus leaves, and several drops of oil to the water and let it soak for at least half an hour. Strain out the spent herbs and discard. Pour the Eucalyptus-water into a container and submerge the rag until it's soaked. Wring the rag out and use it to rub along the chest and neck area. Repeat as needed until your sinuses begin to clear.

Chapter 5
Pain Relief

Reduce Back Pain
{Healing Bath}
13
Components: Dried Lavender Flowers

To help ease back pain, prepare Lavender-water, to be poured into your bathwater. Boil a few cups of water and remove it from the heat. Add a handful of dried Lavender flowers. Cover the pot and let it steep and cool for about half an hour. When the mixture has cooled, then strain out the spent herbs. Pour the strained lavender-water into a warm bath and soak for about ten minutes.

Reduce Arthritis Pain & Discomfort
{Healing Bath}
#14
Components: Lavender, Rosemary, and Tea Tree Oils, and Epsom Salts

Prepare a healing bath by blending 6 drops Lavender oil, with 4 Drops Rosemary oil and 2 drops Tea Tree Oil. Blend the oil mixture with 2 cups Epsom salt, and pour into your bath water. Soak for 15 minutes while concentrating on the pain dissolving as the salt crystals dissolve around you.

Eases Headaches & Migraines
{Aromatherapy & Healing Bath}
15
Components: Dried Lavender, and Lavender Oil

For a soothing Lavender bath to ease your headache away, you'll need to boil several cups of water. Remove it from the heat and add a handful of dried Lavender flowers and several drops of Lavender oil. Cover the pot and let sit for about half an hour. Strain the flowers out of the water and pour the Lavender-water into your warm bath. Slip in and relax for half an hour. You can also rub several drop of Lavender oil onto your shoulder and neck area after you've removed yourself from the bath.

Alleviate Headaches
{Aromatherapy & Folk Magic}
16

Components: Fresh Mint Leaves, or Mint Oil

Another method to try and dispel headaches is to rub fresh mint leaves onto your forehead.

Headache Relief
{Stone Magic}
17

Components: Rose Quartz Stone

To help fight off a headache, place a rose quartz stone underneath your pillow before bedtime or while you rest.

Relieve Physical Stress
{Healing Bath & Aromatherapy}
18

Components: Lavender Oil, Rosemary Oil & Epsom Salts

Prepare a healing bath to ease physical stress on your body by blending six drops Lavender oil, with four Drops Rosemary oil. Blend all but a few drops of the blend with two cups Epsom salt, then pour into your bath water. Slip in and soak for about half an hour, while concentrating on the stresses melting away. When you get out of the bath, rub the remaining few drops of oil onto your shoulder area. If you have sensitive skin, you may want to blend the oil with a lotion or crème before applying directly to your skin

Relieve Pain from Broken Bones
{Healing Compress}
19

Components: Dried Comfrey Leaves and rag

To prepare a Healing Compress for broken bones, sprains, or muscle tension, gather together a handful of dried Comfrey leaves then add it to several cups of boiling water. Remove from heat and let steep for half an hour. Strain out the herbs and discard. Place the rag in the comfrey-water and wring the cloth out gently. Then place the cloth on the afflicted portion of your body. Freshen the cloth every few minutes by placing it back in the infusion, and gently wringing it out. Repeat this for about a half an hour.

Chapter 6
Muscle Complaints

Ease Muscular Pain
{Aromatherapy & Folk Healing}
20
Components: Lavender Oil

Prepare a warm bath and add several drops of Lavender oil into the water. Soak in the water for half an hour. Rub several drops of Lavender oil into affected area.

Ease Muscle Aches, Sprains & Torn Ligaments
{Healing Compress}
21
Components: Dried Comfrey Leaves

To prepare a healing compress for muscular discomforts or sprains, gather together a handful of dried Comfrey leaves then add it to several cups of boiling water. Remove from heat and let steep for half an hour. Strain out the herbs and discard. Place the rag in the comfrey-water and wring the cloth out gently. Then place the cloth on the afflicted portion of your body. Freshen the cloth every few minutes by placing it back in the infusion, and gently wringing it out. Repeat this for about a half an hour.

Eases Muscle Cramps & Relax the Body
{Healing Tea}
22
Components: Dried Valerian Root

To combat internal muscle cramps and relax your body all over, prepare a cup of Valerian Root Tea. Boil one cup of water, then remove from heat. Add one teaspoon of dried Valerian Root and let steep for about fifteen. Strain the spent herb from the tea and discard in your garden. Sweeten your tea with honey or sugar to your liking.

Note: if you have cats or dogs, use caution when preparing and drinking this tea, as they both are strongly drawn to the smell of Valerian. My pets go nuts, but DO NOT let your pets drink this tea!

And, *you* shouldn't use Valerian either, if you're taking *any* medications, without first speaking with your doctor. Adverse reactions might occur when taken with Valium, Xanax, Anti-depressants, and St. John's Wort, so please consult with your doctor.

Relaxes Stiff Neck
{Healing Compress}
23
Components: Oregano

To prepare a healing compress for a stiff neck, boil about four cups of water and add about four tablespoons of dried oregano. Remove it from the heat and let steep for about half an hour. Strain out the spent oregano. Once the oregano-water has cooled, you can saturate the rag, lightly wring it out, and use it to wipe around your neck and shoulders. Repeat this for about a half an hour.

Prevent Backache
{Folk Magic}
24
Components: Dried Mugwort

An old method used to prevent backaches is to carry Mugwort with you. This can be dried Mugwort in a sachet, or fresh Mugwort. This was traditionally used by travelers to ward of aches during their long journeys.

Ease Muscular Tension
{Healing Tea}
25
Components: St. John's Wort

To combat various forms of muscle tension, prepare yourself a cup of St. John's Wort Tea. Boil one cup of water and remove from heat. Add one teaspoon of dried St. John's wort and let it steep for about fifteen minutes. Strain out the spent herbs and discard in your garden. Sweeten your tea with honey or sugar to your liking.

Note: Do not take St. John's Wort if you are taking *any* medications, without first speaking with your doctor.

Chapter 7
Female & Family Concerns

Regulate Menstruation
{Folk Remedy Healing Tea}
26
Components: Mugwort Tea

A folk remedy to regulate an irregular menstrual cycle indicates that drinking Mugwort tea might help resolve your issues. Boil one cup of water, then remove it from the heat. Add one teaspoon of dried Mugwort leaves and let it steep for about fifteen minutes. Add sugar, honey, or other sweetener to your liking. You should drink one glass of the Mugwort tea before bedtime, for about a week.

Note: You should NOT use Mugwort if you might be pregnant, or if you're trying to get pregnant, or if you're breastfeeding.

Remove Stretch Marks
{Healing Magic}
27
Components: Sunflower Oil

To help ease stretch marks after pregnancy, use a drop or two of sunflowers oil and apply to the affected areas.

To Conceive a Baby
{Folk Magic}
28
Components: Sunflower Seeds.

A folk Magic remedy believed to help a woman conceive a child indicates that she might be helped by eating sunflowers seeds everyday as a snack.

Conceive a Baby
{Folk Magic}
29

Ingredients: Small wooden doll, in the image of an infant or child.

For this African based Folk Spell, you'll need a small wooden doll or poppet in the form of a baby or child. It should always be carried with her, in a pocket or purse.

Stop Spousal Abuse
{Aromatherapy & Folk Magic}
30
Components: Lavender Oil

If anyone find themselves in a physically abusive relationship, the ONLY solution is to leave. Family counseling is great, if it's an option, but most abusive people won't go voluntarily. If you're tired of the abuse, and your partner won't seek help, you need to plan your exit strategy.

In the meantime, if you want to pacify your partner until you've made arrangements to leave, try Lavender oil to help provide a calming aroma in the home. You can also wear Lavender oil as cologne around your partner, until you've made arrangements to leave. Because you need to leave. Aggression escalates, whether its mental abuse or physical abuse. If you don't stop the cycle, it continues and grows with momentum. I'd also recommend the strong binding spell to go along with the Lavender. Bindings are found are found in Chapter twenty-five.

Ease PMS (Premenstrual Syndrome)
{Aromatherapy & Folk Magic}
31
Components: Lavender & Rosemary Oils, Epsom Salt

To help ease the monthly discomforts from PMS, try a relaxing healing bath with Rosemary and Lavender Oils. Blend 6 drops Lavender oil, with 2 Drops Rosemary oil. Blend half of the oil blend with 2 cups Epsom salt, and pour into your bath water. Soak for half an hour. When you get out of the bath, rub the remaining oil mixture onto your body. If you have sensitive skin, you may want to blend the oil with a lotion or cream before applying directly to your skin.

Increase Breast Milk Flow
{Folk Magic}
32

To increase breast milk flow, you might find drinking Fenugreek tea helpful. Many mothers report their milk supply doubled after incorporating Fenugreek into their daily diet while breastfeeding. Pre-formulated teas and supplements are the best way for nursing mothers to take in Fenugreek products.

Ease Symptoms of Menopause & Hot Flashes
{Folk Remedies}
33
Components: Flaxseed & Black Cohosh

To help ease menopausal symptoms, Flaxseed and Black Cohosh have both been proven useful in reducing hot flashes. Pre-formulated teas and supplements are the best ways to take in these herbs for the optimal results.

Restless Child
{Aromatherapy & Healing Bath}
34
Components: Dried Lavender Flowers

Want to calm down your child. Try a lavender bath made with lavender-water. To prepare a calming bath gather together 1/2 cup dried Lavender Flowers, and 3 cups of water. Boil the water then remove from heat. Place the dried Lavender flowers in the water and let steep for half an hour. Strain out the spent herbs out and pour the lavender water into a warm bath for your child. Please note, your child's ill temper may be the result of a more serious problem, so if the symptoms persist for more than a day or two, you should consult your physician.

Note: Do not replace the Lavender-water with Lavender oil. Do not use Lavender oil on children.

Lavender, by Shawna Bowman, 2001.

Personal Notations

Chapter 8
Insomnia

Eases Insomnia
{Aromatherapy}
35
Components: Bergamot Oil

Ease yourself to sleep with the relaxing scent of Bergamot oil by placing a few drops of oil on a rag for inhaling the aroma. You can also place a few in an aromatherapy diffuser. If you enjoy the scent, you can add several drops to your bathwater before you retire for bed.

Eases Insomnia
{Healing Tea}
36
Components: St. John's Wort Tea

Many prefer St. John's Wort for battling insomnia. Boil one cup of water, remove from heat, then add one teaspoon of dried St. John's Wort. Let it steep for about fifteen minutes, then strain out the spent herbs. Add sugar, honey, or other sweeteners to your liking. Drink up, and crawl into bed.

Note: Do not use St. John's Wort if you are taking any medications, or using any other herbal supplements, without first speaking with your doctor.

Eases Insomnia
{Candle Magic & Aromatherapy}
37
Components: Blue Candle, and Lavender Oil

A Folk Spell to combat insomnia can be performed with a blue candle and Lavender oil. Anoint the candle with several drops of the oil, then light it. Wait several minutes until wax begins to pool at the top, then add several more drops of the Lavender oil. Let the candle burn for at least an hour or longer before retiring for bed. Make sure to extinguish it before nodding off to sleep!

Eases Sleeplessness & Stress
{Healing Tea}
38
Components: Dried Valerian Root

Valerian Root has many uses, but it's most known for its sleep-inducing qualities. Boil one cup of water, then remove from heat. Add one teaspoon of dried Valerian Root and let steep for about fifteen. Strain the spent herb out and sweeten your tea with honey or sugar to your liking.

Note: if you have cats or dogs, use caution when preparing and drinking this tea, as they both are strongly drawn to the smell of Valerian. My pets go nuts, but DO NOT let your pets drink this tea!

And, *you* shouldn't use Valerian either, if you're taking *any* medications, without first speaking with your doctor. Adverse reactions might occur when taken with Valium, Xanax, Anti-depressants, and St. John's Wort, so please consult with your doctor.

Eases Insomnia
{Healing Tea}
39
Components: Chamomile Tea

A time-honored and ancient method of combatting insomnia suggests that you might have a warm cup of chamomile tea before bed. Boil one cup of water and remove from heat. Add one teaspoon of chamomile and let it steep for about fifteen minutes. Add honey, sugar, or other sweeteners to your liking,

Induce Sleep
{Aromatherapy}
40
Components: Jasmine Oil, & a Rag or Napkin

The scent of Jasmine has been used Asians since to fight insomnia since ancient times, and today Jasmine is celebrated around the world for its sweet peaceful scent. Place a few drops of Jasmine oil on a rag and keep it next to your pillow. Occasionally hold the rag to your face and inhale its scent to help relax both the mind and both.

Induce Sleep
{Folk Magic Healing Tea}
41

Components: Dried Passion Flower leaves

Despite its name, Passion Flower has calming properties and it's been used for ages by North American natives to relieve stress, calm nerves, and as a treatment for hysteria and epilepsy. Recent studies indicate Passion Flower oil an effective treatment for anxiety, so keep your eye on this herb as more studies are conducted.

To utilize it as a sleep aid, boil one cup of water and remove from heat. Add one teaspoon of dried passion flower leaves and let it sit for about fifteen minutes. Remove the spent herbs and sweeten the tea to your liking with sugar, honey, etc. Drink half an hour before bedtime.

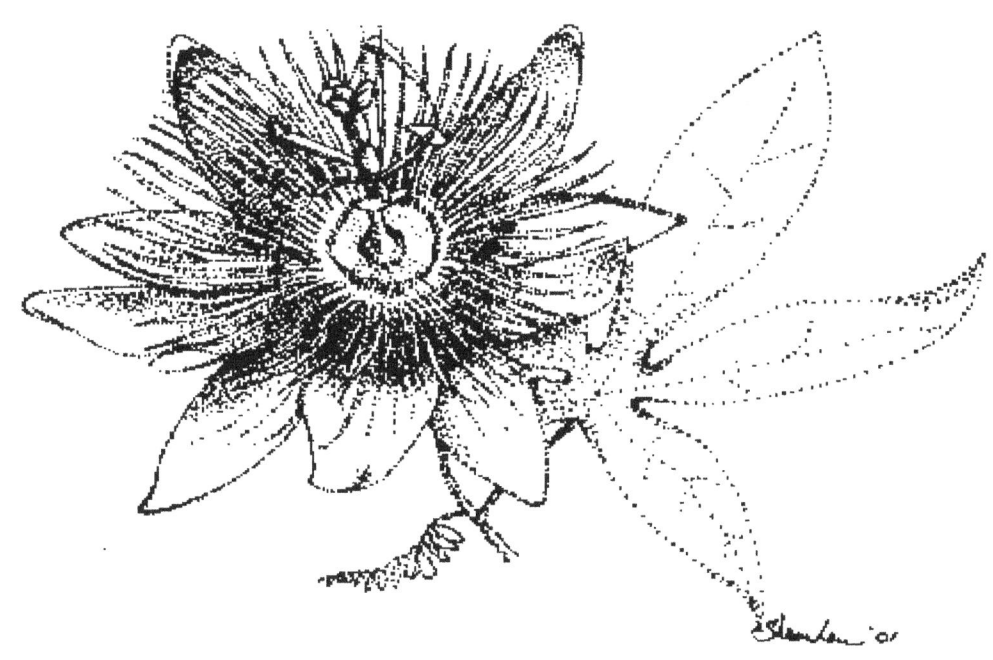

Passion Flower, by Shawna Bowman, 2001.

Personal Notations

Chapter 9
Skin Ailments

Minor Burns
{Topical Healing Application}
42
Components: Aloe Vera

To help ease the symptoms of a painful burn and to promote increased healing, apply Aloe Vera gel to the affected area, several times a day. Any Aloe Vera gel will work, but the fresh harvested gel from an Aloe Vera leaf are ideal. You can use the pulp from one leaf for several days if you refrigerate it after cutting.

Ease Burn Symptoms
{Topical Healing Application}
43
Components: Tea Tree Oil

To help ease the painful stinging sensations produced from burns, you can try applying a drop or two of Tea Tree Oil onto the affected area. If you have sensitive skin, you may want to blend the oil with coco butter before applying.

Ease Painful Cold Sores
{Topical Healing Application}
44
Components: Tea Tree Oil

Tea Tree oil is handy to have around for its antiseptic qualities. It's used for a variety of skin issues including, cold sores, acne, cuts, scrapes, insect bites, and as noted previously, burns. To help get rid of a pesky cold sore, dab a drop of Tea Tree oil on the affected area.

Help Eliminate Acne
{Topical Healing Application}
45
Components: Rosemary Oil, & Lavender Oil

To help get rid of unwanted acne, you might blend 1 drop each of Lavender and Rosemary Oil. Blend the oil mixture with a few tablespoons of a light facial cream and apply the mixture to your face in the morning and evening.

Pimples
(Topical Healing Compress}
46
Components: Patchouli Oil

To get rid of acne, some use a patchouli compress. Get a rag or towel and submerge it warm water, then wring it out. Apply a drop or two of Patchouli oil and cleanse the affected area with the rag. Freshen the rag with warm water and oil as needed.

Skin Rejuvenator
{Topical Healing Application}
47
Components: Rose Oil & Rosemary Oil

To rejuvenate your skin, you might try blending one drop each of Rose and Rosemary oils. It's said to even out skin tones, helping balance both dry and oily skin types. If you have sensitive skin, you may need to blend this with a teaspoon of lotion, crème, or coco butter.

Rosemary, by Shawna Bowman, 2001.

Ease Blisters
{Topical Healing Application}
48
Components: Eucalyptus Oil

To help ease painful blisters, simply rub a drop or two of Eucalyptus Oil onto the affected area. If you have sensitive skin, you may want to blend the oil with coco butter before applying directly to your skin.

Ease Painful Boils
{Healing Topical Application}
49
Components: Jojoba Oil

Used by Natives in Mexico and the Southern U.S, Jojoba oil has been used for years to promote the healing of a variety of skin ailments, including boils. Apply a drop or two to the affected area once a day.

Athlete's Foot
{Topical Healing Application}
50
Components: Lavender Oil & Tea Tree Oil

To help ease the discomforts of Athlete's Foot, rub a drop or two of Lavender Oil or Tea Tree Oil onto the affected area. You may even try a blend of both oils. If you have sensitive skin, you may want to blend the oil/s with coco butter before applying directly to your skin.

Insect Repellent
{Topical Healing Application}
51
Components: Patchouli Oil

Want to be left alone at that picnic, but don't have bug spray? Rub a drop or two of Patchouli Oil onto your skin or clothes before venturing out.

Soothe Insect Stings
{Topical Healing Application}
52
Ingredients: Tea Tree Oil

To help ease the painful stinging sensations produced from ants, mosquitoes, bees, wasps, and other intrusive bugs, you can rub a drop or two of Tea Tree Oil onto the affected area. If you have sensitive skin, you may want to blend the oil with coco butter before applying directly to your skin.

Bursitis
{Topical Healing Application & Healing Bath}
53
Components: Lavender Oil

To help ease bursitis, prepare yourself a Lavender Bath by dropping three or four drops of Lavender Oil into your bath water. Slip in and soak for about half an hour. When you get out of the bath, rub a drop or two of the Lavender Oil onto the affected area. If you have sensitive skin, you may want to blend the oil with coco butter before applying directly to your skin.

Reduce Swelling
{Topical Healing Compress}
54
Components: Jojoba Oil & Rag

Jojoba, as I noted previously, has many uses beyond easing boils. It's also great for reducing inflammation. Add several drops to your bathwater for an al-over soak or put a few drops in a container of warm water and use a rag to wipe down the affected area for localized treatment of a small area.

Ease Swelling
{Topical Healing Compress}
55
Components: Dried Oregano

Some find an oregano compress an affective method for reducing swelling. Prepare a tea by boiling two cups of water and removing it from the heat. Add two tablespoons of oregano and let it sit for about fifteen minutes. Strain out the spent herbs and submerge the rag into the tea. Wring out the rag, leaving it slightly wet, and apply the rag to the affected area. Freshen the rag and repeat for half an hour.

Blackheads
{Healing Compress}
56
Components: Comfrey Leaves and Roots

To remove blackheads, you might try this method which is perfect for use as a compress, or as a facial wash. Boil two cups of water and remove it from the heat. Add in two teaspoons of Comfrey leaves and roots, then let it step for about half an hour. Strain out the herbs and discard. Place the rag in the comfrey-water and wring the cloth out gently, then use it to wash your face, or as a compress. Freshen the cloth every few minutes and repeat several times.

Personal Notations

Chapter 10
Stomach Ailments

Ease Irritable Bowel
{Healing Tea}
57
Components: Valerian Root Tea

To combat irritable bowels, or an upset stomach, you can prepare a cup of Valerian Root Tea to settle your sour stomach. Boil one cup of water and remove from heat. Add one teaspoon of dried Valerian Root to the water and let it steep for about fifteen minutes. Strain out the spent herbs and sweeten with sugar or honey to your liking.

Note: This is a very strongly scented and powerful herb, for which Valium has its origins. Use caution when taking Valerian, as it may cause drowsiness. Also, as mentioned previously, you should use caution when preparing and drinking this tea around pets, as they're drawn to it. Do NOT let your pets drink the tea. Avoid taking with St. John's Wort and Passion Flower. Do not take Valerian Root if you are taking any medications or supplements without first speaking with a doctor or pharmacists.

Heartburn & Nausea
{Healing Tea}
58
Components: Mint

Ease the symptoms of heartburn with a warm cup of Mint Tea. Boil one cup of water and remove from heat. Add one teaspoon of dried mint leaves and let it steep for about fifteen minutes. Strain out the spent herbs and sweeten to your liking with sugar or honey. Mint has been used for many generations to soothe digestion, which eventually evolved into the tradition of the after-dinner mint that we have today.

Ease Cramps
{Aromatherapy}
59
Components: Lavender Oil

Apply a few drops of Lavender oil to your hands and neck area as you would cologne. Many believe the scent acts as an aromatic pain reliever and eases tension in the stomach and abdomen.

Ease Stomach Discomforts
{Healing Tea}
60
Components: Basil

Gather 2 teaspoons of dried Basil leaves and 1 cup boiling water. Remove the boiling water from the heat add one teaspoon of dried Basil. Let it steep for about fifteen minutes then strain out the herbs. Add sugar, honey, or other sweetener to your liking.

Heartburn & Nausea
{Healing Tea}
61
Components: Apple Cider Vinegar, Honey, Ginger Root

My absolute favorite folk drink, Switzel, also called *Switchel*, is super-easy to make and perfect for those who want to take advantage of Apple Cider Vinegar's healing qualities on a regular basis. In a glass, add one tablespoon of Apple Cider Vinegar, one tablespoon of Honey, and a sprinkle of powdered ginger (or a small sliver of fresh ginger root). Blend the three together until well mixed. Traditionally it's served cold, so you can fill the rest of the glass with ice water and mix, starting with about one cup of water. From there, you might need to adjust the flavor more to your liking by adding more water, cider, or honey. Use hot water instead of ice-water for warm and tangy non-alcoholic drinks during cold winter evenings.

Basil, by Shawna Bowman, 2001.

Constipation
{Healing Magic}
62
Components: Dandelion Roots

To ease constipation, cook dandelion roots and leaves, similar to the way you would cook cabbage or spinach, though they may cook quicker. Season the roots with lemon, salt and pepper to your preferred taste. If you're gathering wild dandelions roots, I can't urge you enough to use a reputable site for making your identification in the wild. Misidentification of wild crafted herbs can be deadly. Make sure you know what you're picking.

Personal Notations

Chapter 11
Emotional Strain & Stress

Relieve Tension
{Healing Tea}
63
Components: Dried Valerian Root

Valerian Root, mentioned previously for insomnia and stomach complaints, is also a wonderful tension reliever. You can drink a glass of Valerian Tea before bedtime, or during extremely stressful situations. Boil one cup of water, then remove from heat. Add one teaspoon of dried Valerian Root and let steep for about fifteen. Strain the spent herb out and sweeten your tea with honey or sugar to your liking.

Note: Do not use Valerian if you're taking *any* medications, without first speaking with your doctor. Adverse reactions might occur when taken with Valium, Xanax, Anti-depressants, and St. John's Wort, so please consult with your doctor. If you have cats or dogs, use caution when preparing and drinking this tea, as they both are strongly drawn to the smell of Valerian. My pets go nuts, but DO NOT let your pets drink this tea!

Reduce Tension & Stress
{Aromatherapy & Candle Magic}
64
Components: Lavender Oil, Purple Candle

Gather together one purple candle, and a few drops of Lavender oil. Anoint the candle by rubbing it with a few drops of the oils, while concentrating on the desired effect. Light the candle and let it burn several minutes, until the wax at the top of the candle has melted into a small pool, then pour a few more drops of the oils into the melted wax. Keep the candle nearby as it burns, so that you can benefit from the scent as it permeates the room. If you enjoy the scent, feel free to burn the candle for as long as like.

Anxiety & Depression
{Healing Tea}
65
Ingredients: Dried Passion Flower

To suppress depression, many find Passion Flower useful. Gather together 2 teaspoons of dried Passion Flower leaves and 1 cup boiling water. Remove the boiling water from the heat and put in the Passion Flowers. Let this soak for about 10 minutes. Strain out the spent herbs and add sugar, honey, or other sweetener to your preferred taste.

Mental Balancing & Depression
{Aromatherapy & Healing Bath}
66
Components: Dried Lavender

To help stabilize moods and ease symptoms of depression, prepare yourself a Lavender Bath. Boil about two cups of water and remove from heat, then add about half a cup of Lavender and let it steep for about fifteen minutes. Remove the Lavender and pour the mixture into a warm bath. Relax for about half an hour, periodically taking a moment to deeply inhale the Lavender aroma around you.

Anxiety & Depression
{Healing Tea & Folk Magic}
67
Components: Dried St. John's Wort

St. John's Wort is an excellent mood mender and is one of nature's mood stabilizers. To prepare a healing tea, gather 2 teaspoons of dried St. John's Wort and 1 cup boiling water. Remove the boiling water from the heat and a teaspoon of dried St. John's Wort. Let this soak for about 10 minutes. Add sweetener to your preferred taste.

Tame a Temper
{Aromatherapy & Folk Magic}
68
Components: Basil Leaves

Need to tame someone's temper? Or maybe you need to relax a little yourself, well, cook up some Italian food, and go extra heavy on the Basil. Or, you can prepare a cup of Basil Tea, which is also good for stomach discomforts, although the smell is particularly useful for relaxing nerves.

Nervousness
{Aromatherapy & Folk Magic}
69
Components: Sandalwood Incense

To ease nerves, light a stick, cone, or charcoal tablet of dried Sandalwood incense. Sandalwood's peaceful aroma will help calm those frayed nerves and ease tensions. You can also throw a drop or two of Sandalwood oil into a diffuser for the same effect.

Combat Irritability & Soothe Your Nerves
{Aromatherapy & Healing Tea}
70
Components: Dried Chamomile

Relax irritated nerves with a calming mug of warm Chamomile tea. Boil one cup of water and remove from heat. Add a teaspoon of Chamomile and let it steep for about fifteen minutes, then strain out the herbs. Sweeten with honey or sugar to your liking.

Ease Nervous Headaches
{Healing Tea & Folk Magic}
71
Components: Oregano

To get rid of a nervous headache, you might try eating foods with a lot of oregano, or drink a warm cup of oregano tea. Boil one cup of water and remove from heat. Add in a teaspoon or two of dried Oregano and let it steep for about fifteen minutes. Add sugar, honey, or other sweetener to your liking.

Eases Insomnia
{Healing Tea}
72
Components: Dried Chamomile

In addition to helping to relax nerves, Chamomile is also used to help induce sleep for those suffering from insomnia. Boil one cup of water and remove from heat. Add a teaspoon of Chamomile and let it steep for about fifteen minutes, then strain out the herbs. Sweeten with honey or sugar to your liking.

Personal Notations

Chapter 12
Other Mentionable Healing Methods

Lower Blood Pressure
{Healing Tea}
73
Components: Rosemary

To help lower blood pressure, some find incorporating Rosemary into their diet to be helpful. One might prefer a cup of Rosemary tea. Boil one cup of water and remove from heat. Let it steep for about fifteen minutes then remove the spent herbs. Add sugar, honey, or your preferred sweetener to your liking.

Weight Loss
{Folk Magic}
74
Components: Rosemary Tea

In addition to lowering blood pressure, Rosemary is also believed useful by some to promote weight loss. Boil one cup of water and remove from heat. Let it steep for about fifteen minutes then remove the spent herbs. Add sugar, honey, or your preferred sweetener to your liking.

General Healing
{Folk Magic, Poppet}
75
Components: Cloth Material, Dried Eucalyptus Leaves, Needle & Thread

For general healing purposes, a Healing Poppet stuffed with dried Eucalyptus leaves can be made using the instructions from Chapter Two. The doll should be made from a piece of clothing or a cloth from the ill person. An old sock or a rag will work. When it comes time to stuff the doll, do so with dried Eucalyptus leaves. Once the doll is completed, it should be kept in a safe place where it will not be seen, such as under the bed, or in a closet.

Good Health
{Folk magic}
76
Components: Eucalyptus Leaves

Carrying Eucalyptus is believed by some to help ward off illnesses. You can make a charm bag or sachet filled with Eucalyptus leaves as described in Chapter Two, with blue cloth if it's available. Keep it with you in a pocket or purse, or near the bed. It will also come in handy if you have nasal or lung congestion. Hold the sachet close and inhale the aroma for boost to your breathing.

Healing
{Folk Magic & Aromatherapy}
77
Components: Eucalyptus Twigs or Branches

Along the same lines as the sachet above, some people hang Eucalyptus twigs (with many intact leaves) above a bed to promote healing and general good health. Eucalyptus oil is also might also be used in a diffuser for the same effect.

Diabetes
{folk magic}
78
Components: Garlic

To help combat Diabetes, some find it helpful to eat foods heavily spiced with garlic. If you find the flavor unappealing, you can try garlic pills or tablets.

Garlic Bulb, Shawna Bowman, 2001.

Maintain Sobriety
{Folk Magic}
79
Components: Amethyst Stone

Amulets serve as an old sobriety amulet, still used today in some circles. Those seeking help with sobriety can carry an amethyst stone in their pocket or purse.

Reduce Intoxication
{Folk Magic}
80
Components: Almonds

This is a fun old wives' tale to reduce intoxication. It's said if you eat six almonds before each alcoholic drink, it'll minimize intoxication.

I can picture folks in the past passing out almonds at parties, hoping to keep the rowdiness down. While I don't think there's any truth to this old wives' tale, eating *anything* will increase your metabolism, causing your body to process the alcohol quicker. I don't know that almonds will increase the effect better or worse than any other food.

Note: DO NOT attempt to sober yourself up with almonds before driving. This is an old wives' tale included for fun and chronicling purposes only.

Healing
{Folk Magic}
81
Components: Rosemary

Prior to performing healing Magic, some will wash their hands with a Rosemary infusion. Boil two cups of water and remove from heat, then add a teaspoon of dried Rosemary or a drop or two of Rosemary oil. Let it sit uncovered for about fifteen minutes, then strain out the spent herbs and discard them. Take care to let the infusion continue to cool until its comfortable to touch. Once the infusion has cooled and its comfortable to touch, use it to wash your hands and any tools that might need it before any healing ceremony or spell work performed.

Poison Prevention
{Folk Magic}
82
Components: Black Sachet, & Mugwort

Worried about getting poisoned by someone? An old wives' tale says you might carry a black sachet filled with dried Mugwort leaves. Keep it in your pocket, purse, or near your bed as you sleep.

Long Life
{Folk Magic & Aromatherapy}
83
Ingredients: Lavender

If you want to extend your years, some folks say you should smell Lavender as often as possible, as its supposed to make you live longer with every scent.

Mouth Sores
{Healing Gargle}
84
Components: Rosemary, Sage, and Thyme

To ease the symptoms of a sore throat, mouth sores, or sore gums, you might try gargling twice a day with this infusion. Boil two cups water and remove from heat. Add half a teaspoon of dried sage, half a teaspoon of thyme, and one teaspoon Rosemary. Let it steep for fifteen minutes then strain out the spent herbs. Wait until cool before using. You can store unused infusion in the refrigerator for later use.

Toothache or Mouth Pain
{Healing Application}
85
Components: Clove Oil

An old, but effective method of lessening mouth, gum, and toothache pain is to dab Clove oil (less than a drop) onto the affected area with a cotton swab. Clove Oil is very strong and should be used sparingly and with caution. Too much oil in the mouth will cause salivating, gagging, and will be uncomfortable.

Ease a Grumpy Baby
{Healing Tea}
86
Components: Dill

Dill has been used for years for its calming effect, and unless there is an allergy, it's safe for babies and children. You might try either a dill-tea pop-sickle, or a pickle juice pop-sickle.

For the **Dill Tea Pops**, boil two cups of water and remove from the heat, add in a teaspoon of dried dill and let it steep for about half an hour. Strain out the spent herbs and discard them. Sweeten the tea with sugar or corn syrup, NOT honey. Honey can be very harmful to infants and small children. Pour the tea into pop-sickle molds and freeze.

For a tangier treat, you might try **Pickle Juice Pops.** Mix equal parts pickle juice with water, then sweeten with sugar or corn syrup.

Increase Your Energy
{Folk Magic}
87
Components: Vanilla Bean

Some believe eating or smelling Vanilla Beans will increase your energy levels and promote positive feelings. You might tote a Vanilla Bean in your pocket, purse, or wallet, or one might make a sachet using several beans. The same effect can be achieved by adding a few drops of true Vanilla oil to a candle or diffuser, or by burning incense made with true Vanilla oil or crushed vanilla beans.

Healthy House
{Healing Incense}
88
Components: Dried Thyme

Burning Thyme is an old method to promote a healthy home. Thyme scented incense cones and sticks might be hard to locate, but you can easily make your own by adding Thyme oil to unscented cones or sticks. You can also apply dried Thyme (from your neighborhood grocery store) to charcoal tablets. Thyme oil might also be used in an oil diffuser or atomizer for the same effect.

Quick Recovery of Illness
{Candle Magic}
89

Components: 1 Blue Candle, Rosemary Oil, & Sandalwood Oil

To promote a speedy recovery for someone stricken ill, you might grab a blue candle, Rosemary and Sandalwoods oils. Anoint the candle by rubbing it with a few drops of the oils, while concentrating on the desired healing effect. Light the candle and let it burn several minutes, until the wax at the top of the candle has melted into a small pool, then pour a few more drops of the oils into the melted wax. Keep the candle nearby as it burns, so that you can benefit from the scent as it permeates the room. If you enjoy the scent, feel free to burn the candle for as long as like.

Potent Fertility Sachet
{Folk Magic}
90

Components: Green Sachet, Small Purple Goddess Idol, & Dried Patchouli

This reputedly potent fertility spell calls for carrying a green sachet filled with dried patchouli, with a small purple idol of the Goddess tucked inside. The idol might be made of paper, clay, even plastic. Keep it close, in a pocket or purse, and near the bed.

Fertility Spell
{Folk Magic}
91

Components: 1 Green Candle, A Few Drops of Patchouli Oil

This super easy fertility spell should be performed prior to sexual intercourse. Anoint a green candle with a drop or two of patchouli oil. Light the candle and wait several minutes until wax begins to pool at the top. Place a few more drop of Patchouli oil in the melted pool. For added potency, you might consider adding a drop of Dragon's Blood oil.

Regulate Blood Sugar
{Folk Healing}
92
Components: Apple Cider Vinegar

To regulate blood sugar, some might incorporate a tablespoon or two of Apple Cider Vinegar into their regular diet, either through salad dressings, or as a drink diluted with water. Coincidently, when used as a salad dressing, it helps kill off any Ecoli that might remain on fruits and vegetables, both cleaning it and adding a little tang. Apple Cider Vinegar is a handy tool in your pantry.

Personal Notations

Part III
Spiritual Enlightenment

Divination, Pendulums, & Rune Stones
Prophecy, Visions, & Dreaming
Meditation & Astral Travel
Cleansings, Blessings, & Purifications
Seeking Knowledge & Truth

Chapter 13
Divinations, Pendulums, & Rune Stones

Divination

Divination, or looking into the future, is a practice common among many cultures, including Wiccans. There are hundreds of divination methods found around the world in all cultures. Crystal balls, tea leaves, tarot cards, rune stones, palm reading, and many other methods serve as tools for many who are looking for help with decision making, or for those seeking clues about their future.

Some find pendulums to be an easy, simple, and fun way to decipher the future. You don't even need to draw a chart, just hold the pendulum and track the movements. You must remain relaxed. If the pendulum begins to swing in a direction, let the answer reveal itself. If the pendulum begins to swing in a circle, you should stop, and state your question again, more precisely if possible. Regardless of the tools you use for divination, you will find many helpful hints for enhancing your abilities within the spells found in the remainder of the book.

Pendulum Chart for
Yes & No Issues

Runes

Runes, and similar devices, have been used for thousands of years in various cultures. The runes described here are Germanic in origin, and stem from an ancient writing system. Runes used today vary in styles, symbols, alphabets, and interpretations. The method I describe for you here is the method I've used for the past twenty years. My methods *will* differ from more recent online interpretations. If you dabble with runes and find you enjoy them, there are dozens of great of books on the market you can peruse to get a variety of perspectives from other practitioners. As you learn various methods and the different interpretations, I encourage you to go with what you feel comfortable with. Find a set of runes you love, and find interpretations that speak to you.

My methods are based on the Futhark alphabet, and are divided into three groups called Aetts. These Aetts consist of the Frey's Aett, the Hagal's Aett, and the Tyr's Aett, and are named after Norse deities. The Frey's Aett represents the first eight runes of the alphabet. The Hagal's Aett represents the ninth through the sixteenth runes in the Futhark alphabet. The Tyr's Aett represent the last eight runes in the alphabet. For reference, I've listed under each rune the Aett to which it belongs. In the past, each rune represented either a sound, or a pictorial representation of words, in much the same way the as the Ancient Egyptians. When used to represent sounds, they were used together to form words. Used alone, they represented nouns, people, places, and concepts.

Today, runes come in a variety of unique shapes and sizes and you'll find them carved into stone, wood, bone, antler, or pressed into metal or resin, like coins. They are usually carried in a small bag or box. My husband bought me a necklace years ago with a set of small metal runes threaded onto it, for wearable runes on the go, and it's since become my favorite set, proving that functional sets truly do come in all shapes and sizes.

For each symbol, there are multiple meanings, depending on how it's being used. For the purposes of divination, each rune has a prophetic meaning, with another meaning if the rune is inverted. An inverted rune is one that land upside-down, (wrong-side up) after being casted. To cast runes, I place them in a bag and pull them out one at a time, without looking at it. I then lay or drop it on the table. If the rune lands right-side up, you will see the rune symbol. If the rune lands with its rune-side facing down, it's considered inverted. As you pull the stones from the bag and lay them on the table, place them in chronological order, according to the layout you've chosen, with the inverted runes placed right-side up, but horizontally to signify the inversion. The number of stones pulled from the bag will depend on the size of the layout. I've included several of my personal layouts to get you started. These are found immediately following the rune stone interpretations.

Fehu (Feoh)

Freyr's Aett
Hieroglyphic meaning: Cattle
Equivalent Alphabetic Letter: F

Prophetic Meaning:
Financial gains or wealth.
Inverted (upside down) Meaning:
Loss of money, debts, or ill spent money.

Uruz (ur)

Freyr's Aett
Hieroglyphic meaning: Wild Bison
Equivalent Alphabetic Letter: U

Prophetic Meaning:
Extravagant gain, or the receipt of something special.
Inverted (upside down) Meaning:
The loss of something substantial worth to you.

Thurisaz (Thorn)
Freyr's Aett
Hieroglyphic meaning: Thorn
Equivalent Alphabetic Letters/sound: th

Prophetic Meaning:
A persistent problem, issue, or person.
Inverted (upside down) Meaning:
Someone is helping you, but for the wrong reasons.

Ansuz (Ansur)
Freyr's Aett
Hieroglyphic meaning: Mouth
Equivalent Alphabetic Letter: A

Prophetic Meaning:
Speaking your mind, telling something.
Inverted (upside down) Meaning:
You know something, but you should keep quiet.

Raido (Rad)

Freyr's Aett
Hieroglyphic meaning: Wheel
Equivalent Alphabetic Letter: R

Prophetic Meaning:
Changes made, as in work, life.
Inverted (upside down) Meaning:
Unwise changes.

Kano (Ken)

Freyr's Aett
Hieroglyphic meaning: Torch
Equivalent Alphabetic Letter: K

Prophetic Meaning:
A helpful friend, old or new.
Inverted (upside down) Meaning:
A not-so helpful friend, with ulterior motives.

Gebo (Gyfu)
Freyr's Aett
Hieroglyphic meaning: Gift
Equivalent Alphabetic Letter: G

Prophetic Meaning:
The giving or receiving of a notable gift or present.
Inverted (upside down) Meaning:
The loss of something notable.

Wunjo (Wyn)
Freyr's Aett
Hieroglyphic meaning: Happiness
Equivalent Alphabetic Letter: W

Prophetic Meaning:
Good news or positive information.
Inverted (upside down) Meaning:
Bad news, or negative information.

Hagalaz (Hagal)
Hagal's Aett
Hieroglyphic meaning: Hail
Equivalent Alphabetic Letter: H

Prophetic Meaning:
Shocking news, loss, or damage.
Inverted (upside down) Meaning:
Betrayal from someone you trusted.

Nauthiz (Nyd)
Hagal's Aett
Hieroglyphic meaning: Essential
Equivalent Alphabetic Letter: N

Prophetic Meaning:
A need for something quickly.
Inverted (upside down) Meaning:
Something you don't need.

Isa (Is)
Hagal's Aett
Hieroglyphic meaning: Ice
Equivalent Alphabetic Letter: I

Prophetic Meaning:
Stagnation, something is not progressing, but needs to.
Inverted (upside down) Meaning:
Changes are occurring but require thought.

Jera (Ger)
Hagal's Aett
Hieroglyphic meaning: Harvest
Equivalent Alphabetic Letter: J

Prophetic Meaning:
A decision made quickly.
Inverted (upside down) Meaning:
A decision carefully made.

Eihwaz (Eoh)

Hagal's Aett
Hieroglyphic meaning: Yew Tree
Equivalent Alphabetic Letter/sound: ei

Prophetic Meaning:
End of old habits, beginning something new, enlightenment.
Inverted (upside down) Meaning:
Old habits and ways are restricting progress.

Perth (Peorth)

Hagal's Aett
Hieroglyphic meaning: Chances
Equivalent Alphabetic Letter: P

Prophetic Meaning:
Taking responsibility.
Inverted (upside down) Meaning:
Expecting others to take responsibilities.

Algiz (Eolh)
Hagal's Aett
Hieroglyphic meaning: Elk
Equivalent Alphabetic Letter: Z

Prophetic Meaning:
Experiencing important, notable success.
Inverted (upside down) Meaning:
A need to overcome an obstacle in order to achieve notable success.

Sowelu
Hagal's Aett
Hieroglyphic meaning: Sun
Equivalent Alphabetic Letter: S

Prophetic Meaning:
Receiving much-needed guidance and listening.
Inverted (upside down) Meaning:
Receiving much-needed guidance, and *not* listening.

Teiwaz (Tyr)

Tyr's Aett
Hieroglyphic meaning: God
Equivalent Alphabetic Letter: T

Prophetic Meaning:
Seeking justice, successfully.
Inverted (upside down) Meaning:
Seeking justice for the wrong reasons,
Seeking justice, but not finding it.

Berkana (Beorc)

Tyr's Aett
Hieroglyphic meaning: Goddess
Equivalent Alphabetic Letter: B

Prophetic Meaning:
A Recovery or sudden realization.
Inverted (upside down) Meaning:
Searching for a resolution to a situation.

Ehwaz
Tyr's Aett
Hieroglyphic meaning: Horse
Equivalent Alphabetic Letter: E

Prophetic Meaning:
Carrying too many burdens.
Inverted (upside down) Meaning:
Carrying too many burdens that aren't yours to carry.

Mannaz (Man)
Tyr's Aett
Hieroglyphic meaning: Mankind
Equivalent Alphabetic Letter: M

Prophetic Meaning:
Regretting something you should move beyond.
Inverted (upside down) Meaning:
Not regretting something that you should.

Laguz (Lagu)
Tyr's Aett
Hieroglyphic meaning: Water
Equivalent Alphabetic Letter: L

Prophetic Meaning:
A stable time of physical, spiritual, or financial healing.
Inverted (upside down) Meaning:
Unstable times, physically, spiritually, or financial.

Inguz (Ing)
Tyr's Aett
Hieroglyphic meaning: The God Ing
Equivalent Alphabetic Letter/sound : ng

Prophetic Meaning:
Fertility, pregnancy, growth.
Inverted (upside down) Meaning:
Infertility, stagnation, no growth.

Dagaz (Daeg)
Tyr's Aett
Hieroglyphic meaning: Day
Equivalent Alphabetic Letter: D

An opportunity risen should be taken.
Inverted (upside down) Meaning:
A missed opportunity.

Othilia (Odel)
Tyr's Aett
Hieroglyphic meaning: Property
Equivalent Alphabetic Letter: O

Prophetic Meaning:
Obtaining property, a home, vehicle, or financial equity.
Inverted (upside down) Meaning:
Desiring property, a home, vehicle, or financial equity, but having obstacles.

Blank Rune

Prophetic Meaning:
The Blank Rune represents the unknowable and symbolizes what you cannot see. It indicates a need for self-reflection and introspection before acting.

Reading a 3 Rune Layout

① 1 - The Past

② 2 - The Present

③ 3 - The Future

Rune Cross Layout

1 - General Past
2 - Past Situations
3 - General Present
4 - Present Situations
5 - Obstacles Impacting the Present Situations
6 - Strategy to Deal with the Present Situations
7 - Resolution & Outcome of the Present Situation
8 - General Future
9 - Obstacle Impacting the Future Situations
10 - Strategy to Deal with the Future Situations
11 - Resolution & Outcome of the Future Situation

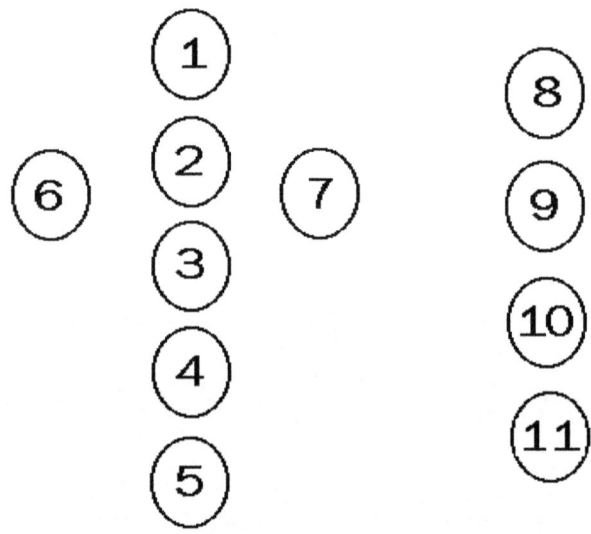

6 Rune Layout

1 - General Past
2 - General Present
3 - Present Obstacles
4 - General Future
5 - Future Obstacles
6 - Resolution & Outcome

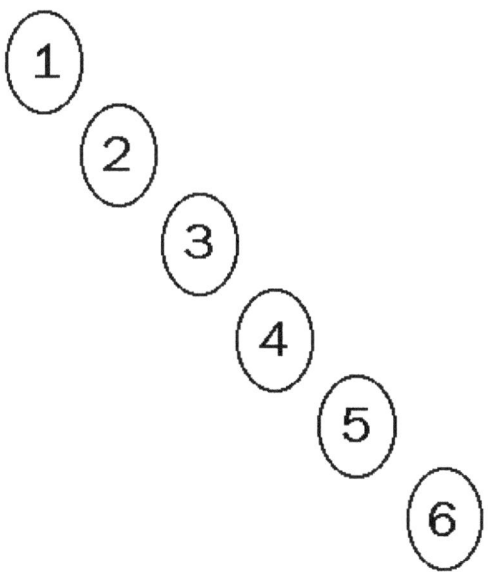

Reading a 9 Rune Layout

1 - General Present
2 - Present Situations
3 - Obstacles Impacting the Present Situations
4 - Strategy to Deal with the Present Situations
5 - Resolution & Outcome of the Present Situation
6 - General Future
7 - Obstacle Impacting the Future Situations
8 - Strategy to Deal with the Future Situations
9 - Resolution & Outcome of the Future Situation

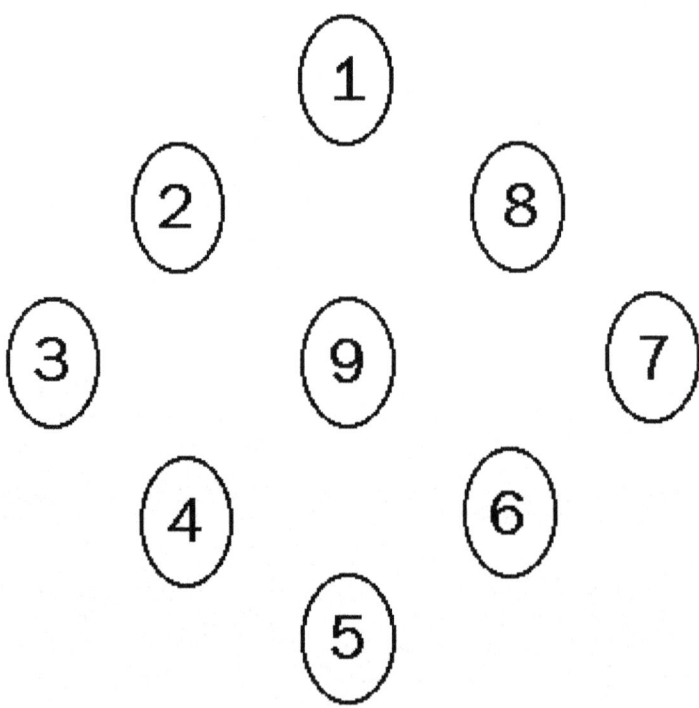

Chapter 14
Prophecy, Visions & Dreaming

Nightmares
{Folk Magic}
#93
Components: Dried Rosemary

A long-used method to help prevent the reoccurrence of nightmares is to place Rosemary under the bed before you go to sleep. If this spell is rooted in aromatherapy, as we might imagine, you might also use Rosemary in an oil diffuser or burn rosemary incense before bed for the same effect of warding off nightmares.

Prophetic Dreaming
{Folk Magic}
#94
Components: Dried Mugwort

If you want to increase the prophetic power of your dreams, some might suggest you place a Mugwort sachet within your pillowcase or underneath your pillow as you sleep.

Divination
{Folk Magic}
#95
Components: Dried Mugwort

Mugwort has a strong association with soothsaying, prophecy, and divination. Some who engage in prophecy seeking might find a cup of Mugwort tea helpful when consumed beforehand. Boil one cup of water and remove from heat. Add one teaspoon of dried Mugwort leaves and let it steep for about fifteen minutes. Strain out the spent Mugwort and sweeten to your liking with sugar or honey. This tea would be appropriate before tarot or rune readings, palmistry, tea leaves, etc.

Prophetic Dreams
{folk magic}
#96
Components: Jasmine Incense

Another method to boost the prophetic power of dreams is to burn Jasmine incense before bed. Jasmine also has calming properties and might help you nod off quicker, too.

Produce Visions
{Folk Magic}
97
Components: Damiana Incense

To increase the likelihood of receiving a *vision* to help with Magical endeavors, some say burning Damiana incense will do the trick. Damiana incense isn't common, so you might want to use dried Damiana leaves with a charcoal tablet. It's advised to burn the incense as you sit within your circle, or near your altar.

Psychic Powers
{Folk Magic}
98
Components: Cinnamon Incense

Cinnamon is another incense some might burn to help increase psychic powers. It's suggested that you burn the incense when you wish to heighten your psychic awareness, during divination sessions, or before bed for prophetic dreams.

Enhance Psychic Powers
{Folk Magic}
99
Components: Sandalwood Incense

Many people prefer Sandalwood during divination sessions to enhance psychic abilities, and it smells better than Mugwort or Damiana, and it's less overpowering than Cinnamon.

Bad Dreams
{Folk Magic & Aromatherapy}
100
Components: Sandalwood Incense

To prevent bad dreams, many employ the scent of Sandalwood. Burn Sandalwood incense before bed to help eliminate upsetting visions while one sleeps. You might achieve the same effect with Sandalwood oil in a diffuser, or with a Sandalwood candle.

Increase Prophetic Power
{Stone magic}
101
Components: Bloodstone Amulet

People sometimes employ the power of Bloodstones to assist in their Magical workings for a variety of purposes, but it's notably used to increase prophetic abilities when the stone is carried or kept close at hand.

Personal Notations

Chapter 15
Meditation & Astral Travel

Meditation Aid
{Folk Magic & Aromatherapy}
102
Components: Frankincense Incense

A wonderful and relaxing incense to aid with meditation is Frankincense. Burn it before and during meditations.

Meditation
{Folk Magic & Aromatherapy}
103
Components: Myrrh Incense

Myrrh is another great incense to burn during meditations. A native to Africa and the Middle East, its warm scent aids with relaxation, concentration, and clarity.

Astral Projection
{Folk Magic}
104
Components: Mugwort Tea

Bump up your astral travel plans with a warm mug of Mugwort tea. Previously discussed as a divination aid, it's also believed by many to increase chances of astral projection while sleeping. Boil one cup of water and remove it from the heat. Add in one teaspoon of dried Mugwort and let it steep for about fifteen minutes. Strain out the spent herbs and add your favorite sweetener and drink up before bed.

Astral Projection
{Magical Sachet}
105
Components: Dried Mugwort

If Mugwort tea isn't your thing, but you still want to utilize Mugwort in your Magical workings as an astral aid, you might try making a sachet with dried Mugwort and keeping it close by the bed, or underneath your pillow before bed.

Astral Projection
{Folk Magic & Aromatherapy}
106
Components: Sandalwood Incense

To help ease into your astral state and for a relaxing out-of-body experience, some say you should burn Sandalwood incense prior to astral travel attempts. Sandalwood's calming scent is believed helpful in creating a calm environment needed to induce an astral state.

Meditation
{Folk Magic & Aromatherapy}
107
Components: Lavender Incense

Meditation might be hard to accomplish if complete peace isn't achieved in your immediate environment. Make sure your meditation area is quiet and pleasant. Lavender incense burned before meditating will certainly help you relax, and some believe it helps one enter a meditative state quicker. As mentioned in previous spells, Lavender's attributes and properties are many, and along with being a meditation tool, it can also help improve your mood, pacify hostilities, ease stress, and maybe get rid of a headache, too. It's versatility and usefulness, along with a perfect scent that balances sweetness with green notes, are why it's a staple in many Wiccan homes.

Potent Meditation Sachet
{Folk Magic}
108
Components: Black Sachet or Bag, 1 Black Obsidian Stone, 1 Clear Quartz Crystal Stone, 1 Turquoise Stone, 1 Moonstone, Dragon's Blood Resin

This reportedly potent sachet is believed by some to be an essential meditation aid, to be kept close by in a pocket or on an altar as one meditates, to strengthen the sessions.

In a black bag, or with black cloth, gather one each of turquoise, black obsidian, clear quartz, and moonstone. Add a teaspoon or two of Dragon's Blood resin, which can be chunks, like small stones, or powdered and poured among the stones within the bag or sachet.

Chapter 16
Cleansings, Blessings & Purifications

Purification
{Ancient Magic}
109
Components: Myrrh

Burning Myrrh is an ancient technique used for purifying objects and is still used today in many parts of the world. Simply pass the object you wish to purify through the smoke of the incense; or, if you want to purify a person, wave the smoldering incense around the bottom portion of the person's body. For homes and large areas, it might be helpful to walk with the incense within the perimeter of the property, allowing the smoke to reach all the areas you wish to purify and cleanse.

Purification Bath
{Folk Magic, Infusion}
110
Components: Dried Lavender

For an easy and beautifully scented purification bath, boil two cups of water and remove from heat. Add a few teaspoons of dried lavender flowers and let it steep for about fifteen minutes. Strain out the dried herbs. Pour the Lavender infusion into a warm bath, then climb in and soak for about half an hour, taking care to clear your mind of negativity as you meditate in the water. If dried flowers aren't available, you might substitute with Lavender oil.

Purification
{Folk Magic}
111
Components: Clove Incense

Burning Clove is another ancient technique used for purifying objects. Pass the object you wish to purify through the smoke of the incense; or, if you want to purify a person, wave the smoldering incense around the bottom portion of the person's body and let the smoke rise for a few moments. For homes and large areas, it might be helpful to walk with the incense within the perimeter of the property, allowing the smoke to reach all the areas you wish to purify and cleanse.

Purification
{Folk Magic}
112
Components: Sandalwood

Native to the Middle and Far East, Australia, and the Pacific Islands, Sandalwood's warm scent remains popular as a purifying scent, just as it was thousands of years ago. As previously noted, simply pass the object you wish to purify through the smoke of the incense; or, if you want to purify a person, wave the smoldering incense around the bottom portion of the person's body and let the smoke rise around them. For homes and large areas, it might be helpful to walk with the incense within the perimeter of the property, allowing the smoke to reach all the areas you wish to purify and cleanse.

Blessing
{Ancient Magic}
113
Components: Frankincense

Burning Frankincense is one of the most popular methods used for Blessing people, objects, homes, and property. Pass the objects through the incense smoke, or to purify a person, wave the smoldering incense around their feet and let the smoke rise around their body. For homes and large areas, walk with the burning incense around and within the perimeter of the property, allowing the smoke to reach all the areas you wish to purify and cleanse.

Blessing
{Ancient Magic}
114
Components: Lavender

My favorite, Lavender, makes a great Blessing tool. The scent is calming, and most people find it pleasant. To purify objects, pass them through the smoke. To purify people, wave the smoldering incense around their feet and let the smoke rise around their body for a few seconds. For homes and large areas, walk with the burning incense around and within the perimeter of the property, allowing the smoke to reach all the areas you wish to purify and cleanse.

Cleansing
{Ancient Magic}
115
Components: Copal (*Protium copal*)

Native to the Americas, Copal's softly sweet scent is reminiscent of Frankincense, but with milder notes. It was used by Pre-Columbian Mesoamerican people as a prized scent in native ceremonial practices. Light the incense and pass the objects through the smoke to cleanse them. To cleanse a person, wave the smoldering incense around the bottom portion of the person's body and allow it to rise up for a moment. For homes and large areas, walk with the burning incense around and within the perimeter of the property, allowing the smoke to reach all the areas you wish to purify and cleanse.

Cleansing Divination Tools
{Cleansing Infusion}
116
Components: Mugwort

Some people find cleansing their tools helpful, and this infusion is specifically for divination tools, such as crystal balls, rune stones, pendulums, and even your hands. Boil one cup of water and remove from heat. Add in a teaspoon of dried Mugwort and let it sit for about fifteen minutes. Strain out the herbs and use the infusion to cleanse and wipe your divination tools down. Some people cleanse their tools before each divination session, while others might only cleanse them during normal dusting and cleaning.

Cleansing
{Cleansing Bath}
117
Components: Dried Chamomile Flowers

Chamomile is a pleasantly scented herb and so it makes a perfect cleansing infusion, leaving you cleansed, calmed, and smelling great. For the Chamomile cleansing bath, boil two cups of water and remove from the heat. Add in two or three teaspoons of dried Chamomile and let it steep for about fifteen minutes. Remove the spent herbs and pour the infusion into a warm bath. While in the bath, visualize negativity leaving, or floating away from you, then replaced with positive light. Concentrate on leaving negativity behind and moving forward cleansed and new.

Anointing Oil
{Jewish Mysticism}
118
Components: Cinnamon Oil & Frankincense Incense

    This anointing oil was reportedly used by Hebrews in the past as a general anointing oil. Simply burn the Frankincense incense and let the open bottle of Cinnamon oil linger though the smoke for a few moments. The anointing oil can be used on candles, tools, other objects as a blessing, cleansing, and purification agent.

Cleansing Magical Knives, Swords, & Athames
{Folk Magic}
119
Components: Onion

    Some believe to consecrate, cleanse, and spiritually prepare your Magical knife, sword, or athame before ceremonial work, you might slice it through a fresh onion beforehand. It would be wise to cleanse the onion juice off the blade after you're finished performing your Magical work. I'd also recommend you apply a light coat of oil to the blade to protect the metal, if you're not doing so already.

Potent Spiritual Awareness Sachet
{Folk Magic}
120
Components: Black Sachet, Dragon's Blood Powder, 1 Hematite Stone, 1 Moonstone, Clear Quartz Stone Crystal

    If you wish to heighten your spiritual awareness, this super easy sachet might come in handy. Gather a black bag or cloth. Inside, place one stone each of hematite, moonstone, and clear quartz crystal. Add in a teaspoon or two of Dragon's Blood powder or several small chunks of resin. The sachet is to be carried or kept close by when meditating, praying, performing Magic, or engaging in a Spiritual act.

Chapter 17
Seeking Truth & Knowledge

Seeking Knowledge
{Folk Magic}
121
Components: Dried Rosemary

If you're looking for knowledge, guidance, insight, or even a lost object, some swear that burning Rosemary incense will help reveal the needed information or insights. Rosemary oil placed in a diffuser would likely achieve the same desired effect. As the scent permeates the room, try to clear your mind for a few meditative minutes. It's believed that the insights and knowledge you seek will be made known to you during your meditations or with within the following days.

Truth
{Folk Magic}
122
Components: Sunflower Blossom

A whimsical approach to gaining insight into the truth of a matter calls for placing a whole sunflower blossom under your pillow before you retire for bed. The knowledge you are seeking will come to you either in the night, or the next day.

Detect another Witch
{Folk Magic}
123
Components: St. John's Wort

A unique spell created for heightening one's awareness, and more specifically, to detect the presence of another witch, is to carry a sachet of dried St. John's Wort with you in your wallet or purse. This is believed by some to heighten psychic senses, too.

Increase Intelligence & Awareness
{Folk Magic}
124
Components: Amethyst

Ancient Egyptians carved scarabs and made beads with Amethyst, and several thousand years later, this beautiful purple stone is still used and highly prized around world. To utilize the properties of Amethyst, simply keep a stone in your pocket.

Spiritual Enlightenment
{Folk Magic}
125
Components: Frankincense

If you're seeking enlightenment, many people suggest using Frankincense resin on charcoal tablets to fill the room with Frankincense incense. You can also use incense cones and sticks made with high quality oils.

Spiritual Awareness
{Folk Magic}
126
Components: Cinnamon

To raise your spiritual awareness, you can burn Cinnamon bark or powder on charcoal tablets to fill the room with cinnamon incense. You can also use incense cones and sticks made with high quality oils.

Potent Enlightenment Sachet
{Folk Magic}
127
Components: Black Sachet, Dragon's Blood Powder or Resin, 1 Hematite Stone, 1 Moonstone, 1 Clear Quartz Stone Crystal, and 1 Amethyst

If you wish to heighten enlightenment, this stone-filled sachet might do the trick. Gather a black bag or cloth. Inside, place one stone each of hematite, moonstone, clear quartz crystal, and amethyst. Add in a teaspoon or two of Dragon's Blood powder or several small chunks of resin. The sachet is to be carried or kept close by when you wish to raise your awareness to achieve enlightenment.

Part IV
General Spells

Protective Measures
Strength and Power
Money
Luck & Wishing
Traveling and Outdoors
Spirits, Ghosts, and Exorcisms
Removing Curses
Other Mentionable Spells

Chapter 18
Protective Measures

Protection Amulet Against Evil
{Folk Magic}
128
Components: Turquoise Stone

If you believe someone is working Magic against you, or if there's other negative forces around you, some suggest that keep a small piece of turquoise stone in your pocket, purse, and by your bed while sleeping.

Protective Amulet
{Folk Magic}
129
Components: Tortoise Shell

People around the world have used tortoise and turtle shells for thousands of years, both decoratively and spiritually. Several Native American creation stories speak of turtles with great reverence, as they carry the world on their shell. Today, shell amulets are worn for protection and to promote good luck. The shell must be from an ethically sourced shell, from an animal that died from natural causes. Many use a tortoise stone instead of shell, for similar purposes, as seen in the previous protection amulet that guards against evil.

Protection from Evil
{Folk Magic}
130
Components: Amber Stone

Some carry an Amber stone with them as protection from evil or to guard off the evil eye. It's believed to repel negativity. Keep it in a pocket, purse, or next to the bed while sleeping.

Protection
{Folk Magic}
131
Components: Chamomile Amulet

To protect homes from negative forces, some people place sachets of chamomile, or hang dried chamomile around the home. It's believed to keep the occupants from being influenced by negative energies.

Drive Away Evil
{Voodoo Magic}
132
Components: Valerian Root

A very potent method of driving away negativity is to burn Valerian Root. The scent is said to provide protection from evil, both physical and spiritual. But, I've gotta warn you. It smells *bad*. Writing this spell made me gag a little - just thinking about a house full of Valerian Root.

So, with that said, in addition to driving away evil, it will drive away most people, too, and as I noted in a previous concoction, it will attract dogs and cats. Which sorta makes it a Magical incense for happy hermits to draw in the neighborhood animals. Which, isn't so bad, if you can tolerate the scent of sweaty, fungus-infected socks that Valerian emits.

Protect Children while they Sleep
{Folk Magic}
133
Components: Garlic Clove

To help protect children as they sleep, some place garlic cloves underneath the bed and in the windowsills. It's believed to protect your little one from negativity, spirits, and nightmares.

Protection
{Folk Magic}
134
Components: Frankincense

An ancient technique, which is still in use today, is to burn Frankincense for protection. Frankincense is one of the most widely used scents and serves as a multi-functional resin, and is appropriate for use during cleansings, for protection, during meditation, and during any spiritual, religious, and Magical workings. Its pleasant aroma is now a staple in many incense blends available around the world.

Protection
{Folk Magic}
135
Components: Myrrh Incense

Another incense burned for its protective properties is Myrrh. You should burn the myrrh in the house or around the property you wish to protect. You can also carry a small bit of myrrh in a bag or sachet and keep it in your pocket or purse, and near the bed as you sleep.

Protection
{Folk Magic}
136
Components: Chamomile Amulet

Another method of obtaining protection from higher forces is to carry Chamomile with you wherever you go. Chamomile incense can also be burned for protection. As noted previously, Chamomile can be hung to dry within the home for protection, too.

Prevent Evil
{Folk Magic}
137
Components: Basil

To protect homes from outside entities after using Ouija Boards, conducting seances, or performing other related spiritual work, some burn sage incense or sage wands afterwards. It serves as both a cleaning and dispelling agent. Some might also sprinkle doorways and windowsills with powdered basil.

Protection
{Folk Magic}
138
Ingredients: Basil Plant, or Basil Stems with Leaves

This fun protection method calls for putting basil in the windows of the rooms you wish to protect. You can use a potted-plant or you can use cut basil placed in a vase with water. The cut basil might spring roots, in which case, plant it and repeat with new stems cut from a different plant. Some people hang dried basil for the same protective qualities.

Lizards
{Folk Magic}
139
Components: Saffron

To keep Lizards from coming into your house, some believe sprinkling Saffron around doors and windows will help ward them off.

Thieves
{Folk Magic}
140
Components: Rosemary Plant

To deter thieves from disrupting a home, some people find it helpful to employ the protective qualities of Rosemary. To keep thieves at bay, one might plant bushes near the doorways and windows of the home.

Fleas
{Folk Remedy}
141
Components: Catnip

You already knew that catnip drives your cat crazy, but it also helps drive flees away. To help protect your cat from fleas, place a few drops of catnip oil in his/her bed, or sleeping area. You can also sprinkle dried catnip in the area.

Protection Against Evil Spirits
{Protective Sachet}
142
Components: Kava Kava Root

To protect against evil spirits, some believe Kava Kava root can help with dispelling negatives forces that might linger around. Fill a bag or sachet with powdered Kava Kava root and keep it in your pocket, purse, or in the home where the entities are active. For large areas, you might make a small sachet for each room.

Protection from Gunshots
{Folk Magic}
143
Components: Pine Cone

For protection against altercations and gunshots, an old wives' tale says you might gather Pine Cones during the Midsummer's Night and eat one nut/seed from it each night until the cone is empty.

Potent Protection Sachet
{Folk Magic}
144
Components: Black Sachet, Dragon's Blood Powder, Hematite Stone, Clear Quartz Crystal, Tiger's Eye, and Turquoise

This protective sachet calls for gathering a black bag or cloth. Inside, place one stone each of hematite, clear quartz crystal, tiger's eye, and turquoise. Add in a teaspoon or two of Dragon's Blood powder or several small chunks of resin. The sachet is to be carried or kept close, in a pocket, purse, or near the bed while sleeping.

Personal Notations

Chapter 19
Strength & Power

Power
{Folk Magic}
145
Components: Dragon's Blood Powder or Resin

If you'd like to add a little extra power to your spell, incantation, incense, or other magic, you might add a little pinch of Dragon's Blood powder or resin to the incense blend, sachet, or herb offering.

Note: DO NOT EAT. Don't ingest, consume, or apply Dragon's Blood to ANY internal or external healing application, tea, or compress.

For Strength in Battle
{Folk Magic}
146
Components: Hematite Stone

Romans and Greeks believed toting Hematite stones with them in battle would increase the wearer's strength and abilities while fighting. The stone might be kept in the wearer's pocket, on a ring, or as pendant on a chain.

Fight Assistance
{Folk Magic}
147
Components: Garlic

Some folks carry garlic, which is believed to increase the carrier's odds during a fight or battle. Small cloves can be tucked away into pockets.

Courage
{Folk Magic}
148
Components: Garlic

As previously noted, garlic might be useful in battles and fights, and so it should come as no surprise that it's also believed to promote courage when eaten before battles and fights. If you're the fighting kind, professionally or leisurely you might eat a meal spiced heavily with garlic before you engage with the opposition, which is believed by many to increase one's courage.

Courage
{Folk Magic}
149
Components: Pine Pollen

Several Native American tribes near or in pine forests once prized these tall giants - and it wasn't because of their wood. Pine trees were also revered for their pollen, which scientists now know is full of testosterone. Natives gathered the pine pollen and kept it in small leather bags, where it was stored until it was needed. Then, when the time came for battle, the natives consumed the pine pollen just before engaging with the enemy.

Today, pine pollen is available in a pill form for those in need of a testosterone supplement. As with any supplement, check with your doctor before using to make sure it's safe for you to use.

Enhanced Spell Power
{Folk Magic}
150
Components: Ginger

To increase one's Magical abilities, or to add potency to ceremonies, many believe eating Ginger Root beforehand will provide a boost and increase results. You might eat Ginger Root, or foods heavily spiced with it, before you perform divination, meditation, or ceremonial Magic.

Enhanced Spell Power
{Folk Magic}
151
Components: Doll, White Feathers, & Dragon's Blood

This neat poppet spell calls for crafting a doll from black material, then filling the doll with white feathers and a dash of Dragon's Blood Resin. Keep the doll hidden, where it's not likely to be found.

Obtain Physical Energy
{Folk Magic}
152
Components: Pennies or Copper

For energy, it's said one might tote a small bag of copper pieces or pennies.

Chapter 20
Money

Gambling
{Folk Magic}
153
Components: Green Dice

Carrying a set of two green dice in one's pocket or purse is said to bring good luck in all gambling matters. The next time you head to the races, or play slot machines, join a card games, or bet on a roulette wheel, throw a couple of green dice in your pocket and see if it makes a difference.

Bring in Extra Money
{Folk Magic}
154
Components: Mint Leaves

To attract money, an old tradition calls for one to carry Mint leaves in a wallet or purse. For extra tips, place mint leaves in your apron if you are a waiter or waitress.

Success with Money Spells
{Folk Magic}
155
Components: Dragon's Blood & Patchouli

To increase one's chance for successful money Magic, some people incorporate a dash or two of Patchouli or Dragon's Blood, or both to incense blends, sachets, or herb offerings.

Note: DO NOT EAT. Don't ingest, consume, or apply Dragon's Blood or ANY internal or external healing application, tea, or compress.

Money
{Folk Magic}
156
Components: Honeysuckle

To increase money flowing into a home, some people might place sprigs of honeysuckle throughout the home. Renew the sprigs periodically to freshen the spell.

Money
{Folk Magic}
157
Components: Fenugreek Seeds

This folk method of drawing money into a home makes you work for it, but people swear by it. Throw a few Fenugreek seeds into the mop bucket with your regular cleaning solution and mop the floors in your home. If you have carpets, you might sprinkle a few seeds along with your regular carpet cleaner before vacuuming.

Money
{Folk Magic}
158
Components: Sandalwood Incense

Some believe burning Sandalwood incense will draw in money and wealth, if burned during the predawn hours, before the sun has risen. Presumably, the same effect might be produced with oils in a diffuser, providing they're used before dawn.

Money
{Folk Magic}
159
Components: Acorn

An old spell used to encourage money to flow your way, calls for you to plant an acorn in the ground, specifically - by the light of the moon.

Potent Money Sachet
{Folk Magic}
160
Components: Black Cloth, Dried Patchouli, 1 Green Quartz Stone,
and Dragon's Blood Resin or Powder

This protective sachet calls for gathering a black bag or cloth. Inside the cloth, place the green quartz stone, a teaspoon or two of Dragon's Blood Powder (or a few chunks of resin) and a few teaspoons of dried Patchouli. Carry the sachet with you and keep it close by while you sleep.

Money
{Folk Magic}
161
Components: Dried Patchouli, Vase, Coins

One of my personal favorite (and most reliable) spells for money centers around the beloved aromatic herb, Patchouli. In a small vase, add several dollar bills and several coins, then fill the remainder of the vase with dried Patchouli. Place the vase somewhere in the home where it will be seen, but not disturbed. Mine are disguised with silk and dried flower arrangements. I occasionally throw extra coins found around the home into mine to keep their Magic active.

Money Vase, by Shawna Bowman, 2001.

Gambling
{Folk Magic}
162

To help with your gambling endeavors, wash your hands in a chamomile infusion beforehand. Boil two cups of water and remove from the heat. Add in a teaspoon or two of dried Chamomile flowers and let it steep for about fifteen minutes. Strain out the herbs and discard the spent pulp. Use the infusion to wash your hands prior to making your bets.

Money
{Folk Magic}
163

Components: Clove Incense

Some people prefer to use clove incense or oils to draw money into homes and businesses. Take care when burning clove as incense. The aroma is strong, and some people do not enjoy its scent.

Money
{Folk Magic}
164

Components: Basil Amulet

Some folks claim using Basil is the way to go when money matters are concerned. Simply carry a few leaves in your pocket or purse. Dried leaves might be placed in a small sachet and kept in your home or car for the same effect.

Finding Treasure
{Folk Magic}
165

Components: Almonds

If you enjoy treasure hunting, you might make your trip more rewarding by placing a few almonds in your pocket before you search. Carry extra almonds for snacking!

To Increase Business
{Folk Magic}
166
Components: Patchouli & Dollar Bill

To increase your profits, grab a dollar bill and place a small bit of dried Patchouli in the middle. Fold the dollar bill up with the herbs inside and wrap the folded bill with green and red twine. For extra power, add a small bit of dragon's blood powder to the patchouli before folding it up.

Personal Notations

Chapter 21
Luck & Wishing

Good Luck
{Folk Magic}
167
Components: Rose Petals

For good luck, gather together a handful of Rose petals, and toss them into your fireplace or campfire for luck. Using the lame premise, you might throw a few rose petals on a charcoal tablet as incense, too.

Luck
{Folk Magic}
168
Components: Sunflower Plants

For good with your plants, you might grow Sunflowers in your garden or around your house. This is supposed to grant the gardener with good tidings and fruitful harvests.

Good Luck
{Folk Magic}
169
Components: Honeysuckle Plants

For good luck you might plant Honeysuckle vines around your home and along the perimeter of your property.

Luck
{Folk Magic}
170
Components: Frankincense Resin

Another method you might employ to increase your luck, calls for a bag of Frankincense resin to be carried in a pocket or purse, and kept close by the bed when sleeping.

Wish
{Folk Magic}
171
Components: Dried Lavender

To encourage one's wishes to come true, it's said that one might place a sprig of Lavender flowers underneath their pillow, before making a wish and going to sleep. It's believed that if you dream about your wish, that it will come true.

Wishing
{Folk Magic}
172
Components: Sandalwood

Sandalwood is believed to help desires and wishes come to pass. To encourage these properties, burn Sandalwood in the evening hours after the sun has set.

Wish
{Folk Magic}
173
Components: Sunflower Plants

It's believed by some that if you make a wish as the sun is setting, while cutting down a Sunflower, your wish will come true if it's in your best interests.

Sunflower, by Shawna Bowman, 2001.

Chapter 22
Traveling & Outdoors

Bad Weather
{Folk Magic}
174
Components: Garlic

To stave off bad weather while camping, hiking, or enjoying the great outdoors, some folks might carry a garlic clove in their pocket to encourage blue skies for the outing.

Safe Traveling
{Folk Magic}
175
Components: Comfrey Root

An easy charm for safe travels indicates you might tie up a few teaspoons of dried comfrey root and carry it tucked in a pocket, purse, or suitcase.

Note: I wouldn't attempt to carry this on a plane. Visually, it might easily be confused for marijuana, and might cause delays as security clears your bag for travel.

Lost Luggage
{Folk Magic}
176
Components: Comfrey Leaves, Lavender Flowers, and Sandalwood

Nothing puts a damper on a trip faster than when your luggage is lost or stolen. To help prevent this from happening, place a small sachet blend in your suitcase, bags, or purse. Tie up a few teaspoons each of Comfrey, Lavender Flowers, and Sandalwood inside a piece of cloth or a small bag. Not only will it help protect your luggage from being lost, your clothes will smell great when you arrive at your destination.

Lightning Strikes
{Folk Magic}
177
Components: Sandalwood

For those who spend a good deal of time outdoors during cloudy or stormy weather, you might make a sandalwood sachet to keep in your pocket or backpack. Some folks place Sandalwood around their home and property to guard against lightning strikes to their homesteads.

Strength
{Folk Magic}
178
Components: Mugwort

When trekking through the woods, one might carry a few slivers of Mugwort inside their shoes, which is believed to increase strength and help prevent fatigue when walking for long periods. Make sure the pieces are tiny and powder-like so their presence within the shoes does not cause discomfort or blistering on your long journey.

Insects Away
{Folk Magic}
179
Components: Patchouli & Tea Tree Oil

To keep bugs away while you enjoy nature, many folks turn to Patchouli and Tea Tree oils. Dab a drop or two of each on your body before heading outside. Keep the oils with you to reapply as you sweat. Also, if you do get bitten, apply a drop of Tea Tree oil directly to the bite or sting to prevent infection.

Keep Away Thunder & Lightening
{Folk Magic}
180
Ingredients: St. John's Wort

To ward off thunder and lightning from one's home, some utilize St. John's Wort by hanging dried branches near doorways and windows, while others keep St. John's Wort sachets tucked in places where they're not likely to be found.

Chapter 23
Spirits, Ghosts & Exorcisms

To Conjure Helpful Spirits
{Folk Magic}
181
Components: Lavender & Sandalwood Incenses

To encourage your chances of summoning spirits, or necromancy, you might burn Lavender and Sandalwood together as you engage in a seance, use a Ouija board, or during any act of contacting the dead, including EVP (electronic voice phenomena) sessions performed by paranormal investigators.

Spirit Summoning
{Folk Magic}
182
Components: Mint Sprigs

Many believe to increase results while communicating with the dead, an offering of mint sprigs should be left out before communications are attempted. During ceremonial and circle Magic, the mint offering should be placed on the altar.

To Dispel Spirits
{Folk Magic}
183
Components: Garlic

Some say, to dispel spirits from your home and property, eat garlic and sprinkle it around the exterior of your property, while some might hang garlic cloves inside the home.

Spirit Help
{Folk Magic}
184
Components: Echinacea

An offering of Echinacea on one's altar is also believed to increase one's abilities to communicate with the dead, and some believe it encourages sprits to stick around, and help you with your other Magical endeavors.

Exorcism
{Folk Magic}
185
Components: Holy Water

Most exorcisms around the world share one component in each of the wildly varied techniques: Holy Water, or as we prefer to call it, Blessed Water. Refer to the instructions in Chapter Two to prepare a batch of Blessed Water. When dealing with the afflicted, remain calm, focused, and determined as the spirit is instructed to leave. Sprinkle the Blessed Water on and around the afflicted individual as the spirit is made to exit. Afterwards, sprinkle the water in doorways and windows.

Exorcism
{Folk Magic}
186
Components: Frankincense Incense

Several cultures might also burn Frankincense to coerce a spirit or deity to remove itself from the victim. Frankincense is believed by many to rid an area of spirits, and cleanse the area of all negativity; however, some use it to *summon* spirits. Taking both uses into consideration, we might assume Frankincense is good for manipulating and controlling spirits, whether to make them show up, or make them leave. It ultimately appears to serve as a way to get their attention and make them listen.

Spirit Calling
{Folk Magic}
187
Components: Lavender Incense, 4 each Black and White Candles

Gather together four black candles and four white candles in the shape of a circle large enough for you to sit or stand within. Light the incense and call to the spirit you are seeking to contact.

Chapter 24
Removing Curses

Remove Curses and Negativity
(Healing Bath}
188
Components: Frankincense Oil

To cleanse yourself of negativity and hexes, you might prepare yourself a Frankincense Bath by adding a couple of drops to your bathwater. Slip in and soak for about half an hour, while visualizing the negativity leaving your body.

Evil Eye
{Folk Magic}
189
Components: Dried Lavender Flowers

If you believe you might be under attack from an evil eye, you can carry a sachet of dried Lavender with you wherever you go. You can also wear Lavender oil as a cologne for the same desired effect of dispelling the evil eye.

Dispel Evil and Negativity
{Folk Magic}
190
Components: Dragon's Blood Incense

To dispel negativity and to keep evil at bay, burn Dragon's Blood resin or powder. Many believe it will also break curses and prevent evil spirits from entering a home. If Dragon's Blood resin or powder is not available, you can use incense sticks or cones for the same effect.

Remove Curses
{Folk Magic}
191
Components: Blessed Water

To remove curses or any negativity, many prefer using Blessed Water, as detailed in Chapter Two. Once you've prepared the Blessed Water, sprinkle it around your house, property, car, and maybe even your work place.

Banish a Person From your Property
{Voodoo/Witchcraft}
192
Components: Picture of Person, & Twine or String

To banish a person from your property and keep them from returning, take a picture of the person, wrap the picture with twine or string until it is completely covered. Bury the picture in the ground where it will not be found. If you wish to remove the banishing, dig up the picture, and untie the twine or string, and bury the picture.

STRONG Binding Spell
{Voodoo/Witchcraft}
193
Components: Picture of Person, Doll, Sand & Rope

A very strong binding spell, meant to be used for protection as well, will work hard magic to keep the intended victim away from you. Make a doll and fill the inside with grass. Place the picture of the person on top of the doll, and wrap the two together with the rope, until neither are visible. Bury the objects in a place far away from where you live, socialize, or work. This spell should only be used for protection purposes, in order to keep faith with the Wiccan way.

Drive Away negativity
{Folk Magic}
194
Components: Frankincense Incense

Burning Frankincense is used to assist in the removal of many types of negativity, evil entities, people, and vibrations. Frankincense burned, is believed to rid the area of all negativity regardless if they are ill tempered spirits, bad natured people, or just negative feelings in an area.

Exorcism
{Folk Magic}
195
Components: Basil

Burning or eating Basil is said to remove any spirits from an area, or a person's body. To prevent a spirit from returning, plant Basil around the property.

Gerard d'Euphrates, Pluto holding Court, 1549. Picture provided by Dover Publications, courtesy of Ernst & Johanna Lehner, from their book, Devils Demons & Witchcraft, 1971.

Drive away Negativity
{Folk Magic}
196
Components: Clove Incense

Another incense burned to dispel general negativity, as well as spirits, people, and negative vibrations is Clove incense. The strong scent is said to force negativity out of the area where the herb or oil is smelled.

Reverse and Send Back A Spell or Curse
{Folk Magic}
197
Components: Pine Needles

If you feel someone has performed Magic against you, you might burn pine needles as you concentrate on repelling the negative energies and forcing them back. This will also aid in blocking future attempts at Magical intrusions. Indoors, you might add a few pine needles to a charcoal burner, or you might use pine oil as you perform your routine cleaning. Outdoors, you might throw pine needles on the campfire.

Chapter 25
Other Mentionable Spells

Ceremonial Relaxation
{Healing Tea}
#198
Components: Dried Kava Kava Root

Native to the Western Pacific Islands, Kava Kava is used by many to promote relaxation prior to or during Native ceremonies. Boil one cup of water and add a teaspoon of dried Kava Kava Root, then let steep for about fifteen minutes. Remove the spent herb and discard. Sweeten the tea with honey or sugar to your liking, and drink on rare or special occasions.

Note: Kava Kava Root use comes with great controversy and it's been banned both in Europe and Canada. There've been several deaths associated with regular consumption of Kava Kava Root. One such case occurred two weeks after a patient began taking daily doses for depression. Most patient death involved kidney and liver failures. So, DO NOT use Kava Kava Root daily, and avoid using Kava Kava with alcohol or if you drink regularly. Also avoid Kava Kava altogether if you have *any* liver or kidney issues.

Youthfulness
{Magical Folk Infusion}
199
Components: Dried Rosemary

To maintain a youthful appearance, some recommend washing your face with a Rosemary infusion, or for a full-body effect, add the infusion to bathwater. To prepare the infusion, boil two cups of water and remove from the heat. As a facial wash infusion, add one teaspoon of Rosemary to the water. For a bathwater infusion, add several teaspoons of Rosemary to the water. Let either steep for about fifteen minutes then strain out the spent herbs. As a facial wash, use the infusion to wash your face and neck as you normally would. As a bathwater infusion, pour it into a warm bath and soak for about half an hour.

Long Life
{Folk Magic}
200
Components: Lavender Flowers or Oil

Some believe that smelling Lavender everyday will increase one's lifespan.

To Make Someone Sympathetic
{Folk Magic}
201
Ingredients: Basil

To encourage someone to be sympathetic to you, some insist that Basil will do the trick. Serve foods heavily spiced with Basil to garner someone's ear and heart.

Lucky House Warming Gift
{Folk Magic}
202
Components: Basil Plant

Basil's properties make it the perfect housewarming gift, as it's believed by many to bring happiness, prosperity, and peace to a home.

Peaceful Home
{Folk Magic}
203
Components: One Bottle, Dragon's Blood Powder, Sugar & Salt

Gather together equal parts Dragon's Blood Powder, salt, and sugar and mix together. Pour the mixture into a bottle and cork or seal it, then place the bottle where it's unlikely to be found by anyone else.

Long Life for a Child
{Folk Magic}
204
Components: A Large Maple Tree

An old folk spell, said to bless a child with longevity, says to pass the youngster through the branches of a Maple Tree to ensure a long life.

Potent Magic Wands
{Folk Magic}
205
Components: Maple Branch

There are many designs for various styles of Magic wands for Witches to choose from, but many believe the wood from a fallen Maple limb to be ideal starting point when crafting a wand of one's own.

Peaceful House
{Candle Magic}
206
Components: 1 Yellow Candle, A Few Drops of Dragon's Blood Oil

To promote a peaceful home, one might burn a yellow candle with a few drops of Dragon's Blood Oil added to the pool of melted wax at the top. It's believed to keep a house happy, healthy, and free from unwanted disturbances. his will help keep your house a happy, healthy, and enjoyable one, free from unwanted, loud upsetting disturbances.

Inhibit Cancer
{Candle Magic}
207
Components: Asparagus, Blueberries, and Sweet Potatoes.

Medical research indicates that diet is an important aspect of fighting any illness, and the same is true for most types of cancer. These foods, asparagus, blueberries, and sweet potatoes are three of the most promising foods to help with one's cancer fight. Make a habit of eating at least one of these foods every day, to help stave off cancer, and maximize your body's natural defenses in fighting it you've been diagnosed.

Personal Notations

Part V
Additional Material & Information

* Essay, *Witch Hunts*
* About the Author
* Bibliography & Recommended Reading

Witch Hunts
An Essay by Dawn Flowers

Historians estimate that around twelve-thousand people, mostly women, have been executed for Witchcraft in the United States and Europe during the last two-thousand years, though most experts agree the number is likely much higher, with undocumented cases far exceeding the twelve-thousand that *were* documented. People are still being charged and executed for Witchcraft in Africa. People were still being charged with Witchcraft in the United States as late as the early 1800's. Witches *today* in the United States are still being harassed by their neighbors, civil, legal, and judicial servants. These are not figurative or metaphorical Witch Hunts. These are people attacked, defamed, and discredited for being Witches. And, one day, it could happen to you. In fact, it's likely that you'll suffer some form of bigotry and discrimination for your religious views at some point in your life. And when you do, you have a choice to make regarding how you'll respond. You can spread the infection by spewing the same type of venom back at them, or you can be kind, and hopefully change people's perceptions about Witchcraft and Wiccans.

Each of those who perished in the colonial Witch Hunts were sacrificed by their communities based on religious texts, by their religious neighbors, spiritual leaders, and religiously infused local governments. I see these same texts mentioned even today a good bit by Christians, Muslims, Witches, Atheists, and others, each looking for reasons to judge, discredit, or hate others. *That* venomous mentality is the *same* mentality that paved the path to the Witch Hunts in medieval Europe and colonial America. Having been in the Metaphysics business for over twenty years, you might imagine correctly that…I've seen some shit. I have *so* many reasons to be bitter. The struggle is real, y'all. I get it, I'm fighting it, and I'm asking, as fellow Wiccans, that you fight it *with* me. When you find yourself criticizing other people's religions, or focusing on how others are screwing up, or how others have things wrong, take a minute. Acknowledge that you have a choice to continue concentrating on others, or to stop and concentrate on improving *yourself,* because you can't do both.

I was raised with several religious influences but took most of my spiritual direction from my grandmother, a devout Southern Baptist for each of her 96 years. My parents are both Christians, as is most of my family. It's out of respect for my elders, my Christian roots, and my family that I extend a general respect to others of the Christian faith. In my home we celebrate both Christian and Pagan holidays, and if we have guests, we'll help them celebrate *their* holidays, too. It's a lot of fun, because that's what happens when people aren't shitting all over each other's holidays, like I see so many do. If you want people to respect *your* religious choices, you must first respect *theirs*, regardless of what they think of yours. Otherwise, you'll both end up missing the Yule/Christmas Combo parties where both Santa and Krampus make appearances. Shit's a lot more fun when we all get along.

I'm going to give you another example, and you might not like it, but stick with me. I love Joel Osteen. Seriously, I do. I love listening to him, and damn it all if he ain't cute, too. But, what I really love about Joel are his messages. He's uplifting. His messages are positive. If you've followed his progress through the years, you'd know that man doesn't have a mean bone in his body, and we've seen him go through it all. Remember when Houston flooded? Hateful memes are still circulating about it, because people don't know any better. But I do, and I think you should, too.

The truth, which in my opinion has never been adequately explained, is complex, and I'm going to give it to you, because not many people looked into the facts before they judged him. If you're not privy to the events, during a flooding event in Houston, Joel was accused of refusing to open his church as a shelter. During and after the flooding event, Joel did a few interviews, and, bless his heart, he didn't do a good job explaining the situation to the angry public's satisfaction. I sat back, cringing, while people who didn't know better judged the man, and I think he even judged himself a little for not erecting a hundred ft. OPEN sign above the church when the rain started.

But the truth is, it wasn't his call. The only reason I know this is because my father managed a civic center, and at various times it was used as a shelter, and so the universe granted me a bit of insight about emergency sheltering and the procedures in place that go along with safely sheltering large crowds. The short of it, it wasn't his call, but he opened his doors anyway. And, despite that – he became the internet's target in typical Witch Hunt fashion.

When events occur that require a large-scale evacuation and sheltering, there are more than a few considerations that must be made. Because supplies can be extremely difficult to maneuver through disaster areas, shelters are opened only as needed, and only if they aren't directly affected by the disaster. Logistically, it makes sense to send supplies to a select few necessary shelters, instead of thirty. There are beds, diapers, pharmaceuticals, food, toilet paper, blankets, clothes, etc. that need to be guaranteed before a shelter can or should be opened to the public. It's the only way to ensure the safety and health of the people being evacuated and sheltered.

Imagine putting ten-thousand people in a room with no assurances of food or medicines. No beds or blankets. No diapers, or enough garbage bags to contain all the soiled diapers. How long do you think ten-thousand people would stay civilized without food or insulin, or if the shelter itself began to flood, all while the youngest and oldest were sitting in soiled diapers? I think the panic would be immediate for some, but it wouldn't take the others long. A few hours would do it for some. Panic spreads like a grass fire, burning up patience and good moods, quickly turning nice, decent people into miserable, angry victims. Between us, that's not the kind of shelter I'd want to stay the night in, nor my children, and it defeats the purpose of having a shelter altogether, considering all of the health hazards within the shelter itself. Garbage containment will be an issue, causing health concerns. Lack of pharmaceuticals for just 24 hours will mean there *will* be deaths, and there needs to be a means to refrigerate or transport the deceased. We haven't even started talking about day two.

In this case, there were major concerns about the church grounds being affected by the flooding. Parts of it had flooded in previous storms, and parts were flooding that time as well. The emergency management teams decided not to use the church as a shelter. Even still, Joel opened his doors to those who came, though there were only a few. There were not crowds of people lined up wanting in. If you walked up, they let you in. Joel's church is a kind church. Had he made a public announcement indicating that the church was open and serving as a shelter, (while being unequipped to handle the thousands of people who would've arrived) it would've created a dire public health concern, complete with the previously mentioned hazards. So, they didn't advertise themselves as being open for sheltering, but they didn't turn anyone away. He's a good guy, and he's got a caring church. And, if I'm going to praise the man, I might should mention that he gives away more money in a year than I'll make in my life, and so I've got no right to call him greedy, and chances are, you don't either.

When Joel's church wasn't designated as an official shelter for evacuees, it wasn't his call, but he opened his doors anyway. He knew the risks, the potential for his church to harbor a mini-disaster unto itself, and he did it anyway, and he provided for those that showed up and needed help. So, if you see a greedy meme about Joel Osteen, I hope you'll think about the whole truth, and not be so quick to judge. Don't make uninformed fun of people, and don't propagate it, or share it. It's the same type of public mockery that incited the Witch Hunts. People making uninformed and often dumbass accusations about someone they *want* to hate, so others will hate them, *too*.

So, be informed, and make your judgements wisely. Instead of focusing on tearing people down, we should focus on building people up. I'm not suggesting you go extreme and start advocating for people you dislike, rather focus on those you do like, and help build them up. Promote your friend's art instead of ranting about the evils of your enemies. When Karma boomerangs back, you want it to feel good when it hits you.

Don't let your hatred or dislike of something or someone become your motivator for action, regardless if it's politics, religion, or your book club. That's not to say you can't be a proud Democrat or Republican, or a proud Wiccan, it just means your focus should be a positive one. Instead of degrading other people, help build *your people* up, whoever that might be.

As the owner of a Metaphysical business for the past twenty years, you might imagine correctly, that I've seen some shit myself. Congregation members from local churches made their rounds to pray on the windows of my storefront. They'd leave handprints behind, and so I'd paid a local homeless man to clean the windows every few days. It bordered on comedic, but it was harassment. If they'd focused their energy directly toward the homeless, instead of me, they could've helped a lot more people. There were a lot of them and united they could have done some good. Instead they spent their time focused on driving out their perceived evil, and the evil of the day depended on what irked the youth group leader that particular week, and I irked him for months, until my online sales exceeded my storefront sales, and I decided to close up shop, which eliminated the bulk of my overhead, and ultimately increased my profits several times over. My husband and I moved to Houston shortly thereafter, to follow an employment opportunity for him, and I ran my business from home, and thought I'd left all opportunities for religious harassment behind. I was so incredibly wrong.

In the months that followed, I garnered a Power Seller ranking on Ebay, where I sold signed editions of my first four books. Business and life in Houston was great, until a most unfortunate incident fifteen years ago, and then life for me in general became difficult, and the events changed the way I look at religion and people. It changed the way I saw everything, and it broke me for a long time.

A child confided to me about abuse that was occurring in her home, and I called the police. One year later, after I reported knowledge of sex trafficking and abuse, I found myself on the witness stand in a court of law, having to explain and justify my personal religious beliefs, when I served as a witness for the State of Texas during the first criminal trial against the two pedophiles I'd reported.

My religious beliefs were scrutinized by the defense attorney, and I had to answer for all the books I'd written, including *this* one, and I had to answer for being a Witch. *Other* trial witnesses were asked about my religious beliefs, which clearly indicated the focus of the trial was no longer about convicting pedophiles, but it'd turned into a bona fide Witch Hunt in a terrifying and real way.

At the time, I felt like my punishment for being a Witch was worse than an execution. I'd have to watch a child get placed back in the home of her sexual and physical abusers, and I'd have to watch pedophiles walk free…because I was a Witch, and *that* discredited my testimony. Knowing that my beliefs and the books I'd written had jeopardized the safety of a child - is a most horrible feeling. It's terrifying, and I'd not wish it on anyone.

When the verdict against the first pedophile came back guilty, I'll admit I was elated, but having been through what I'd just been through left me in a miserable state of confusion. I'd previously thought religious discrimination was illegal, especially where it mattered most - in our judiciary and legal systems, but it's not, or it doesn't matter if it is. This wasn't a case of small-town crap, either. This was in Houston, Texas.

It's been over fifteen years since I had to answer for being a Witch in that Houston courtroom, and though I'd like to think I'm a stronger person for having gone through these things, I wasn't for a long time. They did not make me a better person. They made retreat. I hid in the broom closet. When I finally did start writing again, I wrote in secret, and published in secrecy out of fear that my children would be harassed at school, just as I'd been attacked in that courtroom. I still feel a bit broken at times. Panicked. As far as authors go, I'm incredibly hermetic, which truth be told, encouraged the prolificacy needed to write thirty books under various pen names by the time I was forty. A bittersweet deal, though it made me think about how I view others, and my own tolerances. I found myself much kinder, and certainly more sensitive about Witch Hunts, and not just the ones aimed at Witches, but those aimed at *anyone,* even Joel Osteen.

Even today, extended family members accuse my husband and I of giving our children *cursed* objects. We've had two of our extended family members taken against their will to churches to exercise out their demonic association with us, which I touch on in a recent project, *Help with Hauntings*. For the record, we don't curse objects before we gift them on birthdays *or* holidays.

My point is, I *know* about Witch Hunts. I *know* religious bigotry. I *know* the pain it causes. I know about persecutions. I know about being scared. I know how hateful people can be. I know what *you* know, and I've seen the same shit you've seen. I'm asking you, despite all of that, to join me in rising above it. We can *do* better than that. We can *be* better than that. We can't let other people's judgements, angst, or bitterness turn us into the same judgmental, angsty, and bitter people who sat in judgement of me as a Witch, because they turn into those who sat in judgement of Rebecca Greensmith, for which she gave her life. If you want something to fight for, you can fight against the hate that promote these sorts of non-metaphorical, and very literal Witch Hunts. You can fight it by not succumbing to it yourself. Fight for the right to be kind, and to praise the God and Goddess while you do it. Praise our Father & Mother. Praise the Sun & Moon. Praise Odin & Frigg. Praise Dagda & Dana. Praise Jesus and Mary, Praise Cernunnos & Brigid. Praise any of their names, knowing you can *do* better, and you can *be* better. And in so doing, may your Blessings return thrice over.

    I want to thank you again for your interest in my work, and this additional essay. I hope you found the book useful, and I especially hope you'll consider my pleas within this essay, and you'll work toward spreading tolerance, empathy, and compassion toward others as you journey along the Wiccan path.

~Dawn Flowers, 2019

About the Author

Dawn Flowers is an East Texas writer, born and raised under the shade of the Piney Woods where she resides with her family and pets. She released her first book in 2001 and has since authored and published over thirty books on a wide range of subjects, including both fiction and non-fiction works, under a variety of pen names.

Her non-fiction titles reflect her love of religions, while her non-fiction titles reflect her love of horror. Most noted for her non-fiction metaphysical titles, she's also written and compiled twelve children's books for kids of the Christian, Jewish, and Wiccan faiths. Seven of her works were written and compiled under the name of Dawn Nefer-Aten, and were published for a non-profit, live-action, role-playing group, Amtgard, during her citizenship within the Kingdom of the Wetlands.

Her first fiction project, a short story titled, In the Forest, appeared in an eponymously titled collaborative book project with four other East Texas writers in 2011. The story was later revised into a horror novella. She then went on to write a series of six horror stories for children, with several more currently in the works.

Her most notable non-fiction works include The Book of Dark & Light Shadows and The Spell Book of Wiccan Shadows. Both titles were released online in 2011, and both rose to reach Amazon's #1 Best Seller rank for their categories, including Mysticism, Witchcraft, Paganism, and Neo Paganism. Almost a decade later, both titles continue to teeter within Amazon's top 100 best-selling books within their categories. Several of her titles are now available at Barnes and Nobles.

For a complete list of available titles, bulk offers, or to keep up with new releases and free book offers, you may visit **DawnaFlowers.com**, or follow her on Facebook page: Dawna Flowers Books.

Other Books by Dawn Flowers

Religions & Spirituality
The Book of Dark & Light Shadows
The Spell Book of Wiccan Shadows
The Wiccan Holiday Cookbook
Witch Wars
Help with Hauntings
The Little Wiccan's Set (Coming Back Soon!)

Adult Fiction
In the Forest, Horror Novella
Sea Loot, Horror Novel (Coming Soon!)

Childrens Fiction
Along Came Cthulhu
Bigfoot of the Big Woods
Story of Krampus
Crazy 'Coon Lady
Wolves of Woodsmen County
Helpful Hank
Sally Scratch & the Squirrel (Coming soon!)
The Bat House Bag (Coming soon!)

Bibliography & Recommended Reading

I graciously give thanks to the authors, publishers, photographers, and illustrators of the below cited works for their donations of information, and their significant help with the writing of this book. For further insight into the Magical Arts, I recommend each of the titles noted below. These sources will provide thought provoking insights into a wide variety of metaphysical matters, and I am sure you will enjoy them as I have.

1. Alli, Antero. *Angel Tech*: *A Modern Shaman's Guide to Reality Selection.* California: New Falcon Publications, 1994.
2. Barrett, David. *Runes.* New York: Dorling Kindersley Publishing, Inc., 1995.
3. Broughton, Richard, Ph. D., *Parapsychology: The Controversial Science*. New York: Ballantine, 1991.
4. Bremness, Lesley. *Herbs: The Visual Guide to More than 700 Herb Species from around the World.* New York: DK Publishing, Inc.1994.
5. Cunningham, Scott. *Encyclopedia of Magical Herbs*. St. Paul: Llewellyn, 1994.
6. Dash, Mike. *Boderlands: The Ultimate Exploration of the Unknown.* New York: Dell Publishing 2000.
7. Dubin, Reese P., *Telecult Power: The Amazing New Way to Psychic and Occult Wonders*. New York: Parker Publishing Company, Inc., 1970.
8. Ernst & Johanna Lehner. *Devils Demons & Witchcraft*: 244 Illustrations For Artists and Craftspeople. New York: Dover Publications, 1971. p. ix, 31, 32, 62, 63, 67,   92, 117, 170, 174.
    a. Albrecht *Durer,* The Four Witches,1497.
    b. Rouleu Mortuaire de Saint Vital, Demonic letter T, 12th Century.
    c. Page from Egyptian Book of Dead.
    d. Albrecht Durer, Witch on goat to Walpurgisnacht.
    e. Hans Baldung Grien, Witches Brewing, Strassburg, 1514.
    f. Rembrandt Harmensz van Rijn, Engraving of Faust, 1652.
    g. The Tragicall Histoire of the Life & Death of Doctor Faustus, 1631.
    h. Gerard d'Euphrates, Pluto holding Court, 1549.
    i. S. Tschechonin, Incubi Seducing Girl, 1913.
    j. Jan van der Deyster, Final Page, 1732.
9. Frazer, Sir James George. *The Illustrated Golden Bough: A Study in Magic and Religion.* Abridged by Robert K. G. Temple. New York: Simon & Schuster Editions, 1996.
10. Frazer, Sir James George. *The Golden Bough.* New York:

Macmillan Publishing CO. Inc., 1978.
11. Gonzalez-Whippler, Migene. *The Complete Book of Amulets & Talismans.* St. Paul: Llewellyn Publications, 1998.
12. Hardin, Terri. *Supernatural Tales from Around the World.* New York: Barnes & Noble Books,1995.
13. Janet Bord, and Colin Bord. *The World of the Unexplained: An Illustrated Guide to the Paranormal.* New York: Sterling Publishing Co., 1998.
14. Krieger, Dolores, Ph.D, R.N., *Accepting Your Power to Heal: The Personal Practice of Therapeutic Touch.* New Mexico: Bear & Company Publishing, 1993.
15. Lowman, Shawna. Created and contributed the following works of art:
    a. *Basil*, Ink Drawing. Houston: Under the Moon, 2001.
    b. *Out of Body Experience*, Ink Drawing. Houston: Under the Moon, 2001.
    c. *Candle Dressing*, Ink Drawing. Houston: Under the Moon, 2001.
    d. *Money Vase*, Ink Drawing. Houston: Under the Moon, 2001.
    e. *Wiccan Tools*, Ink Drawing. Houston: Under the Moon, 2001.
    f. *Charcoal Incense Burner*, Ink Drawing. Houston: Under the Moon, 2001.
    g. *Garlic Bulb*, Ink Drawing. Houston: Under the Moon, 2001.
    h. *Passion Flower*, Ink Drawing. Houston: Under the Moon, 2001.
    i. *Making a Sachet*, Ink Drawing. Houston: Under the Moon, 2001.
    j. *Ghost*, Ink Drawing. Houston: Under the Moon, 2001.
    k. *Eucalyptus Leaves*, Ink Drawing. Houston: Under the Moon, 2001.
    l. *Lavender*, Ink Drawing. Houston: Under the Moon, 2001.
    m. *Sunflower*, Ink Drawing. Houston: Under the Moon, 2001.
16. Levi, Eliphas. *The History of Magic.* Translated by A.E. Waite. Maine: Samuel Weiser Inc., 1999.
17. Penguin Productions. Font type face Walrod, A was graciously provided by the Font Foundry and is copyrighted by Penguin Productions, 1992.
18. Ryall, Rhiannon: *West Country Wicca: A Journal of the Old Religion.* Washington: Phoenix Publishing Inc., 1989.
19. Thatcher, Virginia S., Editor. *The New Webster Encyclopedic Dictionary of the English Language.* New York: Consolidated Book Publishers, 1977.
20. Wyley, Graham. *The Illustrated Guide to Witchcraft.* New York: Parkgate Books Ltd., 1998.

Jan van der Deyster, Final Page, 1732. Picture provided by Dover Publications, courtesy of Ernst & Johanna Lehner, from their book, Devils Demons & Witchcraft, 1971.

Made in the USA
Columbia, SC
19 September 2021